# BLOCK SCHEDULE LESSON PLANS

## HEATH

# DISCOVERING FRENCH
## ROUGE

McDougal Littell
A HOUGHTON MIFFLIN COMPANY
Evanston, Illinois • Boston • Dallas

International Standard Book Number: 0-618-09506-3


2 3 4 5 6 7 8 9 0 -MDO- 06 05 04 03 02 01

# CONTENTS

These lesson plans were designed to help both beginning and experienced teachers by providing an overall framework for translating a *Discovering French—Rouge* unit section to a teacher's daily plans.

## Description of the block schedule lesson plans

Each lesson plan follows the same format:

❏ *Objectives* serve to remind the teacher of the communicative, linguistic, and cultural goals of each unit section.

❏ *Motivation and Focus* provides an introduction to the unit section, activating students' background knowledge about topics to be presented, and discussing cultural situations to make comparisons and to link language and culture. *Info Magazines* provide information for browsing and for reflecting on cultural information in attractive and stimulating magazine format.

❏ *Presentation and Explanation* introduces the new material of the unit section. Vocabulary, expressions, and grammatical structures are presented in a cultural context, usually a conversation. Then the separate components are explained, giving students a chance to think critically about the language.

❏ *Guided Practice and Checking Understanding* provides focused practice, from listening comprehension to oral exchanges and readings.

❏ *Independent Practice* allows students to apply vocabulary, expressions, and grammar to communicate their own ideas in role plays, interviews, information gap activities, and reading and writing practice.

❏ *Monitoring and Adjusting* suggests ways teachers can ensure that students understand the language and learn what has been taught.

❏ *Assessment* gives suggestions for formal assessment at the end of each section and unit.

❏ *Reteaching* provides suggestions for helping students who have not mastered the material.

❏ *Extension and Enrichment* provides culture-based activities that give additional practice in reading and writing, as well as extra assignments and projects.

❏ *Summary and Closure* allows students to recall and further assimilate what they have learned in the unit section. The *Lecture* gives students a chance to read for pleasure. The *Lecture* activities also allow students to use critical thinking skills and to make cultural observations. Writing activities give students a chance to express their thoughts and to personalize their language learning experience.

Each unit is organized around a theme. *Info Magazine* contains theme-related cultural and background information that prepares students for the language presented in the unit sections. The first two (one unit has three) sections within a unit develop communicative and linguistic skills. The third (or last) section consists of the *Interlude culturel*, which provides readings and information about historical and contemporary culture.

It is advantageous to use a variety of materials in addition to the **Student Textbook**. The ***Discovering French*** program facilitates this in several ways:

❏ The integrated **Audio** and **Video** (**Audiocassette, Audio CD, Video,** and **Videodisc**) components make it easy to incorporate technology into the program in ways that support and extend the work done with the textbook. The **Audio** provides an opportunity for students to listen to French conversations, to practice listening and speaking skills, and to practice new structures in context. The **Video** is an excellent format for presenting cultural situations and having students comment on similarities and differences between French and American culture. Complete transcriptions of the **Audio** and **Video** sound tracks are available in the **Cassette Script** and **Video Script** books.

❏ The **Extended Teacher's Edition** provides an abundance of suggestions for extension activities, extra projects, cross-curricular connections, and real-world applications. In addition, there are resources and suggestions for using practice activities, cooperative learning, critical thinking, and portfolio assessment. Additional activities, Teaching to Multiple Intelligences, Cooperative Pair Practice, and Interdisciplinary/Community Connections provide projects and research activities along with activities to help teachers reach all students by addressing various learning styles and needs in the classroom.

❏ **Practice Activities** and the **Video Activity Book** provide guided practice exercises, both oral and written, to complement each unit section's goals. Used with the **Audio** or **Video** (or **Cassette Script** and **Video Script**), these activity books lead students from listening comprehension exercises to communicative and critical thinking activities. Written exercises can be used for independent practice. There is a **Teacher's Annotated Edition** of the **Activity Book**; answers to the **Video Activity Book** activities are included in the back of the book.

❏ The **Teacher's Resource Package** provides materials for reteaching, independent practice, and extension and enrichment. Students can monitor and assess their own progress by using the **Answer Key** to check their work. **Teacher to Teacher** gives suggestions, puzzles, and worksheets that reinforce and reteach language, helping teachers reach all students by addressing various learning styles and needs in the classroom. **Internet Connection Notes** allows students to explore and experience the French-speaking world through the Internet.

❏ **Overhead Visuals: Copymasters and Activities** contains complete blackline versions of all overhead visuals. These transparencies can be used to present and practice new vocabulary and structures, and for reteaching and summarizing material. There are also historical time lines for use with the *Interludes culturels* and transparencies that correspond to each of the *Lectures*. The activity section of the book includes a description of each visual, suggestions for review and practice activities, and expansion activities correlated to the national Goals and Standards for Foreign Language Learning.

❏ The **Testing and Assessment Kit** contains **Achievement Tests, Proficiency Tests**, and forms for **Portfolio Assessment**. Achievement tests include **Unit Quizzes, Unit Tests**, and **Reading and Culture Tests and Quizzes**. Proficiency tests for **Listening Comprehension Performance, Speaking Performance**, and **Writing Performance** can be administered at the end of each unit to see how well students can use French to communicate. Portfolio assessment is facilitated by the use of forms for contents, student instructions, and evaluation sheets for both Oral and Written Portfolios.

## Block scheduling

Block scheduling can mean different things in different places. In some versions of block scheduling, classes meet every other day for two semesters ("AB" scheduling). In other versions, classes meet every day for one semester ("4 x 4" scheduling). What all types of block scheduling have in common is that class periods are longer; they are double, or almost double, the length of a traditional period.

Longer periods can provide numerous advantages to foreign language teachers. They allow the kind of intense exposure to the language that helps make immersion teaching so successful. With less time spent on beginning- and end-of-class housekeeping tasks, block scheduling gives students more time on task and facilitates more in-depth coverage of content. Longer periods also give teachers more time to focus students' attention on the language and to provide the practice needed to be able to use the language. Teachers find they have plenty of time for pair and group work without sacrificing explanation and teacher-directed practice. Finally, longer periods allow for extra projects and activities that motivate students to use their new language. Whether it's writing and producing videos, exchanging cultural packages with a French-speaking class somewhere, or producing a French talent show, block scheduling gives teachers the flexibility needed to do the kinds of long-term, hands-on projects that make the language real for students.

Although block scheduling can help foreign language teachers be more successful, teachers working with block scheduling face a challenge. Experienced teachers may find that doing the same activities for longer periods of time does not always work.

Beginning teachers may have a hard time keeping students' attention for 90 minutes at a time. For all teachers, the key to successful implementation of block scheduling is careful planning. Without careful planning, the extra time provided by longer periods is wasted, and the advantages of block scheduling are lost.

In planning for block scheduling, it is helpful to think about the traditional separation of foreign language teaching activities into "skill getting" and "skill using." Skill-getting activities, while necessary, have no authentic purpose beyond practice. They should be short and as varied as possible in order to maintain students' interest. Skill-using activities are things for which students might use the language in the real world; they have an authentic purpose. These activities should take advantage of the longer periods of time that block scheduling allows. Planning for block scheduling should include both shorter, more varied activities (skill-getting), and longer, more intensive activities (skill-using).

In planning both skill-getting and skill-using activities, teachers working with block scheduling will find it advantageous to use the variety of ancillary materials available with the ***Discovering French*** program. One very effective way to do this is to set up a variety of work stations around the room, where students can work independently, in pairs, and in small groups on activities using as many of the following ancillary configurations as possible:

- CD-ROM work stations where students in pairs or small groups can work independently
- Video (or laserdisc) areas where students can view the video several times and do the activities in the Video Workbook
- A class set of Activity Books and a cassette player so that students can do the recorded activities, either as a full class or in a listening area of the room
- Several Answer Keys so that students in triads can do the activities in the Student Text, with two students performing the dialogues and the third student following in the Answer Key and acting as language consultant.

# REPRISE A: *La vie courante*, PAGE XVI

## BLOCK SCHEDULE (1 DAY TO COMPLETE)

### Objectives

**Communication Functions and Contexts**
To talk about favorite activities and vacation activities
To describe oneself and others
To talk about food and beverages

**Linguistic Goals**
To review the use of the present tense of regular verbs and common irregular verbs
To review *être*, *avoir*, *aller*, *faire*, *venir*, and expressions used with these verbs
To review the use of the present tense with *depuis* to talk about what you have been doing
To review regular and irregular adjectives to describe people
To review use of the partitive article to talk about food quantities

**Reading and Cultural Objectives**
To learn how French young people spend their vacations
To review the French-speaking world and its people
To read for pleasure and information

**Note:** *Reprise* is a review of material from **Discovering French–Blanc**. Use the activities to reactivate basic skills, evaluate students' proficiency, and help select reteaching and review activities from *Rappels* 1–8. You may have students do the *Rappel* activities in **Practice Activities** to help assess needs. See the suggestions for pacing on TE pages T28–T29.

### Motivation and Focus

❑   Welcome students and introduce yourself briefly. Invite students to introduce themselves. Ask about vacation or favorite activities. Arrange students in pairs to ask and answer questions. Invite students to introduce their partners to the class.

❑   Ask students to describe the people on pages xvi–3. What are they doing? Where did they go? Share the information in the NOTES CULTURELLES on TE page 1. Read *Thème et Objectifs*, page 1, to prepare for the review activities.

❑   *Vive les vacances!:* Use the TEACHING STRATEGY: WARM-UP on TE page 2 to review expressions for talking about activities. Read pages 2–3 and discuss where the four young people went and what they did. Help students locate the areas mentioned in the readings on **Overhead Visuals** Transparencies 1, 1(o), and 3. Share the information in the NOTES CULTURELLES, TE pages 2–3. Do *À votre avis* and *À votre tour!* on page 3.

### Presentation and Explanation

❑   *Rappel 1 (Bonjour!):* Ask students to suggest words that describe themselves. Guide students to use the words to describe themselves or friends. Use the TEACHING STRATEGIES: WARM-UP, TE page 4, to review *avoir* expressions. Refer students to *Appendix A* pages R7 and R3 if more review of adjectives and *avoir* expressions is needed. Have students look at the cartoon at the bottom of page 5 and describe the sequence of events. Help students talk about what they are going to do, are doing now, and have just done. Students can study page R3 for additional review of *aller*, *être*, and *venir*.

❑   *Rappel 2 (Le temps libre):* Have students read the letter on page 6. Ask about Valérie's favorite activities. Guide students to talk about their own preferences. Review using the present tense + *depuis* + time to describe what you have been doing for some time using the *Rappel!* box, page 6, and the RAPPEL note, TE page 6. Refer students to pages R2–R3 for review of regular and irregular verbs and expressions with *faire*. Do *Et vous?*, page 7.

❑   *Rappel 3 (Bon appétit!):* Have students look at the restaurant ads on page 8 and suggest food that might be available in each of the places. Review names of foods and drinks, *Appendix A* page R11. Talk about foods students like. Share the information in the NOTES CULTURELLES, TE page 8. Review the definite article to refer to things in general and the partitive to refer to quantities of things using the *Rappel!* box, page 8. Students who need additional review of articles and the verbs *prendre* and *boire* can study *Appendix A* pages R6 and R2, and *Appendix C* pages R24–R29. Do *Et vous?*, page 9.

## Guided Practice and Checking Understanding

❏ Check understanding of pages 2–3 with the COMPRÉHENSION questions, TE page 3.
❏ Introduce the **Video** program. Read the introductory paragraph about *Mise en scène* in the **Video Activity Book** and have students do *Préparation* activities A, B, and C.

## Independent Practice

❏ Model the activities on pages 4–9. Have students practice the activities orally in pairs or groups in class and write responses for homework. Do the EXPANSION, TEACHING STRATEGY, and COOPERATIVE PAIR PRACTICE suggestions on TE pages 3, 4, 7, 8, and 9.

## Monitoring and Adjusting

❏ Have students do activities 1–10 on pages 3–10 of **Practice Activities**.
❏ Monitor students' work as they complete the writing activities in **Practice Activities** and textbook practice activities. Refer students to the appropriate *Rappel!* boxes (pages 5–9), *Reference* pages of the textbook, and writing activities in **Practice Activities**.

## Reteaching (as required)

❏ Redo any of the activities in **Practice Activities** after reteaching vocabulary and structures or after students have studied the appropriate sections in the *Appendix*.
❏ Use the EXPANSION activity, TE page 5, to reteach adjectives, and the TEACHING STRATEGY: CHALLENGE on TE page 6 to reteach verb and pronoun forms.

## Extension and Enrichment (as desired)

❏ For expansion activities, direct students to www.mcdougallittell.com.
❏ Students can browse through any of the *Interlude culturel* sections in the textbook.

## Summary and Closure

❏ Review *Vive les vacances!* on pages 2–3. Help students describe the vacations of the four teenagers. Guide them to talk about their own past summer activities. Students can do their own self-assessment of vocabulary and structures that they need to review.
❏ You may want to use the oral activities on page 3 for inclusion in students' Oral Portfolios. The letter in activity 2, page 7, can be used for Written Portfolios (see pp. 2–3 of **Portfolio Assessment**).

## End-of-Section Activities

❏ *À votre tour!:* Choose any or all of the *Situations* on page 10 for students to role play. Students can present their conversations to the class.
❏ *Rappel culturel:* Do the cultural review quiz independently or in pairs. Have students locate the places on maps, *Appendix D* pages R34–R37. Share NOTES CULTURELLES, TE page 11. Use the TEACHING STRATEGY, TE page 11, to review the French-speaking world.

## Assessment

❏ Use the letter that students wrote in activity 2, page 7, to assess writing skills.

# REPRISE B:  *Hier et avant,* PAGE 12

## BLOCK SCHEDULE (1 DAY TO COMPLETE)

### Objectives

**Communication Functions and Contexts**   To talk about clothes to describe people

**Linguistic Goals**   To review the use of the *passé composé* to describe past events

To review the *imparfait* and its uses to describe the past

**Reading and Cultural Objectives**   To review the cultural background of the French-speaking world

**Note:** Select *Rappel* activities based on students' needs. Move quickly through *Reprise*, encouraging students to refer to the *Révision* sections in the *Appendix* of the textbook (see boxes, pages 12–18) for more support.

### Motivation and Focus

❏   Have students look through the pictures on pages 12–18. Encourage students to talk about the different vacation activities pictured. Use the cartoons at the bottom of pages 12 and 13 to guide students to discover the major communicative and grammar structures to be reviewed: talking about past events and *le passé composé.*

### Presentation and Explanation

❏   *Rappel 4 (Le weekend):* Do the TEACHING STRATEGY: WARM-UP, TE page 12, to have the class create a group story describing actions in the past. Then use **Overhead Visuals** Transparencies 10 and 10(o) and the TEACHING STRATEGY, TE page 13, to review vacation vocabulary and talking about past activities. Review formation and use of the *passé composé* in the *Rappel!* box, page 12. Refer students to *Appendix A* page R4 for more review of regular and irregular verbs in the *passé composé*.

❏   *Rappel 5 (En vacances):* Have students read the travel itinerary on page 14. Ask a volunteer to locate Morocco on **Overhead Visuals** Transparency 4. Help students talk about the trip using the *passé composé*. Explain the use of *être* with verbs of movement. Review agreement of the past participle with the subject using the *Rappel!* box, page 15. Refer students to page R4 for review of the *passé composé* with *être*.

❏   *Rappel 6 (Qu'est-ce qui se passe?):* Show **Overhead Visuals** Transparency 11. Guide students to explain the story on pages 16–17. Explain the use of the imperfect tense to describe the circumstances of an event or what you were doing at a past time, using the *Rappel!* box, page 17. Restate the story using the imperfect and *passé composé*, as needed. Students who need additional review of the imperfect can study page R5.

### Guided Practice and Checking Understanding

❏   Use **Overhead Visuals** Transparency 12 and the Review and Practice and Goal 1 activities on page A26 to review clothing vocabulary. Practice using the imperfect with Transparency 13, using the activities on page A27.

❏   Show the Mise en scène section of **Video** Module 1, or read from the **Video Script**, and have students do *Visionnement* activities D and E in the **Video Activity Book**.

### Independent Practice

❏   Model the activities on pages 12–18. You may want to have students practice the activities orally in pairs or small groups in class and then write their responses for homework. Do EXPANSION, TE pages 13 and 15, and the TEACHING STRATEGY suggestions in the side margin of TE page 16.

## Monitoring and Adjusting

❏ Have students do the activities on pages 11–14 of **Practice Activities**.

❏ Monitor students' work as they complete the writing activities in **Practice Activities** and textbook practice activities. Refer students to the appropriate *Rappel!* boxes (pages 12–17), *Reference* pages of the textbook, and writing activities in **Practice Activities**.

## Reteaching (as required)

❏ Redo any of the activities in **Practice Activities** after reteaching vocabulary and structures or after students have studied the appropriate sections in the *Appendix*. Use the TEACHING STRATEGIES, TE pages 14–19, to meet all students' needs.

## Extension and Enrichment (as desired)

❏ For expansion activities, direct students to www.mcdougallittell.com.

❏ Enrichment reading for students who are interested could be any of the *Interlude culturel* sections in the textbook.

❏ Share the REALIA NOTES on TE pages 12 and 14 and the NOTES CULTURELLES on TE page 18. Do the TEACHING STRATEGY: EXPANSION on TE page 14 for additional oral practice in describing "vacations" based on travel brochures and catalogs.

## Summary and Closure

❏ Show **Overhead Visuals** Transparency 13. Have students choose one of the scenes and imagine they were there. Use the Goal 1 activities on page A28 to help students talk about past events and describe scenes. Help others summarize the communicative and linguistic goals demonstrated.

❏ Do the STUDENT PORTFOLIOS suggestion on TE page 19 to record students' conversations based on the *Situations* on page 19.

## End-of-Section Activities

❏ *À votre tour!:* Have the class do any or all of the *Situations* on page 19 for students to role play. Invite pairs to present their conversations to the class.

❏ *Rappel culturel:* Do the two cultural review quizzes on pages 20–21. Use the suggestions in TEACHING STRATEGY, TE page 20. Help students locate places mentioned on maps, using **Overhead Visuals** Transparencies 1–7 or *Appendix D* pages R34–R37. Explain the information in the NOTES CULTURELLES, TE pages 20 and 21.

## Assessment

❏ Assess students' oral skills as they do activities 3 and 4 on page 18.

# REPRISE C: *Nous et les autres,* PAGE 22

## BLOCK SCHEDULE (1 DAY TO COMPLETE)

### Objectives

**Communication Functions and Contexts**
To refer to people, things, and places

To offer, accept, or refuse personal services

To ask for assistance

**Linguistic Goals**
To review the use of object pronouns

To review negative expressions

To review the different use of the verbs *connaître* and *savoir*

To review other irregular verbs: *voir, écrire*

**Reading and Cultural Objectives**
To learn how French young people spend their vacations

To review the French-speaking world and its people

To read a short story for pleasure

**Note:** Do *Rappel* activities as needed, keeping the pace lively and light. Encourage students to refer to the *Révision* sections in the *Appendix* of the textbook (see boxes, pages 22–25) for more support.

### Motivation and Focus

❑    Have students look through the pictures and photos on pages 22–25. Encourage them to read and comment on the cartoons on pages 22 and 23 and the scenes on pages 24–25. Share the NOTES CULTURELLES, TE page 24, about *les romans-photos.* Help students guess the content and goals of the *Reprise.*

### Presentation and Explanation

❑    *Rappel 7 (Vive l'amitié!):* Review object pronouns using the cartoon on page 22. Guide students to find examples of the object pronouns. Explain the information in the *Rappel!* box, page 22. Use the TEACHING STRATEGY, TE pages 22–23, to help students recognize and use direct and indirect object pronouns. For additional explanation, refer them to *Appendix A,* pages R8–R9.

❑    Review the verbs *connaître* and *savoir.* Students can use the cartoon on page 23 to help explain the different uses of the verbs. Model the negative expressions in the *Rappel!* box at the bottom of page 23. Have students repeat. Guide students to use the expressions to talk about people and things they know or don't know. Refer students to pages R8–R9 as needed.

❑    *Rappel 8 (Un garçon timide):* Have students read the **roman-photo** on pages 24–25. Guide them to notice examples of direct and indirect object pronouns. Explain the information about object pronouns in the *Rappel!* box, page 25. You may want to use the TEACHING STRATEGY at the bottom of TE pages 24–25 to demonstrate the need for object pronouns. Refer students to pages R8–R9 for review of object pronouns. Review the verbs *voir* and *écrire.* Help students use these verbs to talk about people they see or write to. Students can study *Appendix C* pages R26–R27 and R30–R31 for irregular verb forms.

### Guided Practice and Checking Understanding

❑    Check understanding of the **photo-roman** using the TEACHING STRATEGY in the side margin of TE page 24.

❑    Review **Video** Module 1. Show the Gros plan section, or read from the **Video Script,** and have students do the corresponding activities in the **Video Activity Book.**

## Independent Practice

❏ Model the activities on pages 23 and 25. You may want to have students practice the activities orally in pairs or small groups in class and then write their responses for homework. Do the EXPANSION activities on TE pages 23 and 25.

## Monitoring and Adjusting

❏ Have students do activities 1–4 on pages 15–18 of **Practice Activities**.
❏ Monitor students' work as they complete the writing activities in **Practice Activities** and the textbook practice activities. Refer students to the appropriate *Rappel!* boxes (pages 22–25), *Reference* pages in the textbook, and writing activities in **Practice Activities**.

## Reteaching (as required)

❏ Redo any of the activities in **Practice Activities** after reteaching vocabulary and structures or after students have studied the appropriate sections in the *Appendix*.

## Extension and Enrichment (as desired)

❏ For expansion activities, direct students to www.mcdougallittell.com.
❏ Introduce the SUPPLEMENTARY VOCABULARY about space and aliens on TE page 23. Then have students create a story ending to the cartoon on page 23. Follow the suggestions in EXPANSION: RAPPEL on TE page 23.

## Summary and Closure

❏ Revisit the *photo-roman* on pages 24–25. Have students retell the story briefly and then create an ending for it. Guide others to summarize the communicative and linguistic goals demonstrated.

## End-of-Section Activities

❏ *À votre tour!:* Choose any or all of the *Situations* on page 26 for students to role play. Students can present their conversations to the class. If desired, record conversations for inclusion in students' Oral Portfolios.
❏ *Lecture (Les trois bagues):* Use the story in *Lecture* to review and reactivate vocabulary and structures, using the TEACHING NOTE, TE page 27. Share the information in the NOTES CULTURELLES, then read and discuss *Avant de lire* to help students make predictions about the story. Have students read the story on pages 27–30 in pairs, stopping to answer the *Avez-vous compris?* questions and do *Anticipons un peu!*. Use any or all of the TEACHING STRATEGIES or TEACHING NOTES on TE pages 28–30. Show **Overhead Visuals** Transparency LR as a visual cue for pairs of students to do the *Dramatisation* and *Situations* on page 31. Have students do any of the *Expression écrite* activities on page 31.
❏ You may want to use any of the STUDENT PORTFOLIOS suggestions on TE page 31 to record oral *Après la lecture* activities or to assess students' writings (see **Portfolio Assessment**).

## Assessment

❏ Use the conversations that students practice in activities 2 (page 23) and 2 (page 25) as an informal assessment of oral skills and use of object pronouns.

# UNITÉ 1: *Au jour le jour, Partie 1,* PAGE 32

## BLOCK SCHEDULE (3 DAYS TO COMPLETE)

### Objectives

**Communication Functions and Contexts**
To describe what a person looks like
To talk about caring for one's appearance

**Linguistic Goals**
To use adjectives to describe people
To use the definite article with parts of the body
To use parts of the body to describe people's ailments
To use reflexive verbs to describe what people do for themselves

**Reading and Cultural Objectives**
To understand the importance of personal appearance for French young people
To understand how artists have expressed the concept of beauty
To read for pleasure

> **Block Schedule**
>
> **Fun Break** Have students bring in fashion magazines and advertisements from the Sunday paper. Students cut out photos of people and paste them onto index cards. Collect index cards and show them to the class one by one. Have students describe both the physical features and the clothing of the people.

---

### DAY 1

## Motivation and Focus

❑ *Unit Opener:* Look at the photos on pages 32–35, read *Thème et Objectifs* on page 32, and predict the theme of the unit. Discuss the importance of looking good. What is important to American teenagers and to French teenagers?

❑ *Info Magazine:* Have students read pages 33–34. Encourage them to read for general understanding, using cognates and guessing meaning from context. Discuss the article using TEACHING STRATEGY: WARM-UP, TE page 34. Read page 35, sharing the NOTES CULTURELLES in the TE margin. Do *Et vous?*, pages 34 and 35.

## Presentation and Explanation

❑ *Le français pratique (La description physique):* Model and have students repeat the expressions in the boxes on pages 36–37. Do the TEACHING STRATEGY: WARM-UP, TE page 36, to help students use vocabulary for physical description.

❑ *Langue et communication (L'usage de l'article avec les parties du corps):* Present the definite article with body parts, page 38, using **Overhead Visuals** Transparency 15 and the overlay, 15(o). Optionally, you may also explain other uses of the definite article in *Allons plus loin*, page 39.

## Guided Practice and Checking Understanding

❑ Use **Overhead Visuals** Transparency 14 and the activities on page A30 to help students practice describing people. Practice toiletry vocabulary with Transparency 16, using the Goal 1 activity on page A34 and the Goal 4 activity on A35.

❑ Have students do pages 107–111 of **Practice Activities** as you play the **Audio**, Cassette 1, Side 1, or read from the **Cassette Script**, pages 1–4.

❑ Review **Video** Module 1. Show *Problème!*, or read from the **Video Script**, and have students do the corresponding activities in the **Video Activity Book**, as well as the *Supplément* activities.

❑ Practice descriptive words with the TPR activity **"Jacques dit"** mentioned on TE page 37.

## Independent Practice

❑ *Pair activities:* Model the activities on pages 37–39. Do 1, 2, and *Conversations libres* (page 37) and 2 (page 39) in pairs. Have students check their work using the **Answer Key**. Do EXPANSION, TE page 37.

❑ *Homework:* Assign activities 1 (page 38) and 3 (page 39).

❑ Do any or all of the additional activities in **Teacher to Teacher**, pages 1–3 or 7–10.

## DAY 2

### Motivation and Focus

❑ Begin the INTERDISCIPLINARY/COMMUNITY CONNECTIONS project described on TE page 55. Help students work in small groups to plan their travel manuals.

### Presentation and Explanation

❑ *Le français pratique (La toilette et les soins personnels):* Use **Overhead Visuals** Transparency 16 to introduce toiletry vocabulary. Model the words in the box, page 42; students can say which items they use. Use TEACHING STRATEGY: WARM-UP, TE page 43, to write a group story.

❑ *Langue et communication (Les verbes réfléchis):* Present the forms and uses of reflexive verbs, page 44. Use the TEACHING STRATEGY: WARM-UP, TE page 44, to help students discover the difference between reflexive and nonreflexive verbs. You may optionally present the stress pronoun + **même** construction in *Allons plus loin*, page 45.

### Independent Practice

❑ *Pair activities:* Model the activities on pages 40–45. Do 2 and 3 (page 43), and 6 (page 45) in pairs. Have students check their work using the **Answer Key**. Do VARIATION and EXPANSION, TE page 45.

❑ Have students read *Entre nous*, pages 40–41. Use any of the TEACHING STRATEGIES, TE pages 40 and 41, and the *Et vous?* questions on page 41.

❑ *Homework:* Assign activities 1 (page 43), and 5 (page 45).

### Monitoring and Adjusting

❑ Have students complete activity 1, page 19, and activities 1 and 2, pages 20–21, of **Practice Activities**.

❑ As students work on these practice activities, monitor use of articles, reflexive verbs, and description and toiletry vocabulary. Refer to the boxes on pages 36–44 as needed. Do the TEACHING STRATEGIES on TE pages 37–44 to meet all students' needs.

## DAY 3

### Reteaching (as required)

❑ Use the *Reference* section of the textbook as needed for reteaching: *Appendix A* pages R2–R3 for present tense of regular verbs; R12 for body parts; *Appendix C* pages R20–R21 for verbs with spelling changes.

❑ Have students do any of the *Pratique* activities in **Practice Activities** as appropriate: pages 19–20 for use of the definite article, and page 21 for present tense of verbs.

❑ Students can use the **Video** program to review portions of the lesson.

### Extension and Enrichment (as desired)

❑ Play the games described on TE pages 37 and 42 to describe famous people and to match objects and actions related to personal care.

❑ For expansion activities, direct students to www.mcdougallittell.com.

❏ Have students do the **Block Schedule Activity** at the top of page 7 of these lesson plans.

## Summary and Closure

❏ Show **Overhead Visuals** Transparency 12. Have students describe one of the people in the picture, while other students guess which person is being described. Then ask students to summarize the language and communication goals demonstrated.

❏ The *Conversations libres* on page 37 could be taped for inclusion in students' Oral Portfolios. Use the suggestions and forms in **Portfolio Assessment**. For Written Portfolios, use the letter to Juliette in *Et vous?* on page 41.

## Assessment

❏ Use the quiz for *Info Magazine* in **Reading and Culture Tests and Quizzes**. Assess understanding of each part of the lesson by administering the **Unit Quiz** for *Partie 1*.

## Notes

# UNITÉ 1: *Au jour le jour, Partie 2,* PAGE 46

## BLOCK SCHEDULE (4 DAYS TO COMPLETE, INCLUDING UNIT TEST)

### Objectives

**Communication Functions and Contexts**
To describe the various aspects of one's daily routine

To express how one feels and to inquire about other people

**Linguistic Goals**
To use the *passé composé* of reflexive verbs

To use reflexive verbs idiomatically

To use the imperative forms of *s'en aller*, *se taire*, and *s'asseoir*

**Reading and Cultural Objectives**
To understand what constitutes the daily routine for different French people

To read for pleasure

To read fiction: a short story by Ionesco

> **Block Schedule**
>
> **Change of Pace** Have students create small posters depicting related reflexive and nonreflexive actions, such as **Je me lave le matin** and **Je lave le chien le week-end**.

---

### DAY 1

### Motivation and Focus

❑ *Info Magazine:* Show **Overhead Visuals** Transparency 17 as you read *À la résidence Bon Repos* on page 46. Have students identify who lives on which floor of the building and in what order they wake up. Do any or all of the TEACHING STRATEGY and FOLLOW-UP activities described on TE page 47, or *Et vous?* on page 47.

### Presentation and Explanation

❑ *Le français pratique (La routine quotidienne):* Model and have students repeat the daily routine expressions on page 48. Do the TEACHING STRATEGY: WARM-UP described on TE page 48 to write a group story using the vocabulary.

❑ *Langue et communication (Le passé composé des verbes réfléchis):* Present the **passé composé** of reflexive verbs, page 50. Do the TEACHING STRATEGY: WARM-UP described on TE page 50 to have students change a group story into the past.

### Guided Practice and Checking Understanding

❑ Use **Overhead Visuals** Transparency 16 with the Goal 1 activity on page A35 to practice talking about daily routines. Use Transparency 18 and the suggested activities on pages A40–A41 to have students practice talking about feelings.

❑ To check listening, use the **Audio**, Cassette 1, Side 2, or read from pages 4–7 of the **Cassette Script** as students do the activities on pages 112–114 of **Practice Activities**.

### Independent Practice

❑ *Pair activities:* Model the activities on pages 49–51. Do activities 1, *Conversations libres* (page 49), 1 (page 50), and 2 (page 51) in pairs. Have students check their work with the **Answer Key**. Do the VARIATIONS on TE pages 49–51.

❑ *Homework:* Assign activities 3–4 on page 51 for homework.

❑ Do any or all of the additional activities in **Teacher to Teacher**, pages 4–6 or 11–14.

## Presentation and Explanation

❏ *Le français pratique (La condition physique et les sentiments):* Model and have students repeat the physical condition and feelings expressions in the box on page 52. Have students ask and answer questions about how they feel.

❏ *Langue et communication (L'usage idiomatique des verbes réfléchis):* Present the idiomatic use of reflexive verbs, page 54. Have students create sentences using the verbs in the *Vocabulaire* box. You may optionally present use of reflexive verbs to express a reciprocal action in *Allons plus loin*, page 54.

## Guided Practice and Checking Understanding

❏ Play the Mise en scène section of **Video** Module 2, or read from the **Video Script**, and have students do the corresponding activities in the **Video Activity Book**.

❏ Drill forms of reflexive verbs with the TPR VERB DRILL, TE page 45, and the TPR CONJUGATION DRILL, TE page 51.

## Independent Practice

❏ *Pair activities:* Model the activities on pages 53–55. Do 1–3 (page 53), and 1–4 (page 55) in pairs. Have students check their work with the **Answer Key**. Do the VARIATIONS on TE pages 49–51.

❏ Do any or all of the additional activities in **Teacher to Teacher**, pages 4–6 or 11–14.

## Monitoring and Adjusting

❏ Have students do activity 1 on page 23, activity 1 on page 24, and the *Communication* activities on page 26 of **Practice Activities**.

❏ As students work on these practice activities, monitor use of reflexive verbs and vocabulary for daily routines and feelings. Refer students back to the boxes on pages 48–54 as needed. Use the TEACHING NOTES, TEACHING STRATEGIES, and NOTES LINGUISTIQUES in the TE margins to help meet all students' needs.

## Reteaching (as required)

❏ Use the *Reference* section, *Appendix C* pages R20–R21, to reteach verbs with spelling changes.

## DAY 3

## Extension and Enrichment (as desired)

❏ Play the games described on TE pages 51 and 55 to use reflexive verbs in the ***passé composé***, and to use idiomatic reflexive verbs.

❏ If desired, have students read for enrichment the Ionesco short story on pages 57–59, or any of the *Interlude culturel 1* selections on pages 60–69.

❏ For expansion activities, direct students to www.mcdougallittell.com.

❏ Have students do the **Block Schedule Activity** at the top of page 10 of these lesson plans.

## Summary and Closure

❏ Show **Overhead Visuals** Transparency 50. Ask students to choose one of the people in the picture and describe what they did on the day of the picture. Have other students summarize the communicative and linguistic goals demonstrated.

❏ *Lecture (Conte pour enfants de moins de trois ans):* Read the description of Ionesco and *Avant de lire* on page 56. Have students read the story on pages 57–59 in pairs, answering the *Avez-vous compris?* questions and doing *Anticipons un peu!*. Share the information on TE pages 56–59: Notes culturelles, Notes linguistiques, Additional Information, and Teaching Strategies. Use the quiz for *Lecture* in **Reading and Culture Tests and Quizzes**. Have students prepare the role plays, page 59, using **Overhead Visuals** Transparency L1 for cues.

❏ You may videotape the role plays for students' Oral Portfolios. See Student Portfolios, TE page 59, and the suggestions in **Portfolio Assessment**.

## Assessment

❏ Use the quiz for *Info Magazine* in **Reading and Culture Tests and Quizzes**. Assess understanding of each part of the lesson by administering the **Unit Quiz** for *Partie 2*.

### DAY 4

## Reteaching (as required)

❏ Have students do the *Pratique* activities on pages 23 and 25 of **Practice Activities** to reteach verbs with spelling changes.

## Assessment

❏ Use **Unit Test 1** after completing the unit's activities. You may also wish to give any or all of the following **Proficiency Tests** for the unit: **Listening Comprehension Performance**, **Speaking Performance**, and **Writing Performance**.

## Notes

# INTERLUDE CULTUREL 1: *Le monde des arts,* PAGE 60

## BLOCK SCHEDULE (2 DAYS TO COMPLETE – OPTIONAL)

### Objectives

**Reading Objectives**   To read for content: information about French modern art

To read poems by Desnos and Prévert

**Cultural Objectives**   To learn about impressionism and impressionist artists: Monet, Degas, Renoir, Manet, B. Morisot

To learn about artists of the post-impressionist era: Van Gogh, Gauguin, Matisse, Rousseau, Toulouse-Lautrec

To learn about surrealism as an artistic and literary movement: Magritte

**Note**: The *Interlude culturel* contains cultural information about French modern art. It can be taught as a lesson or introduced in smaller sections as parts of other lessons. Use the material in this section in any way that meets your needs: to expand cultural awareness, as source material for student research projects, to develop reading skills, or to build cultural knowledge.

### DAY 1

### Motivation and Focus

❏   Have students preview the pictures on pages 60–69. Ask them if they are familiar with any of these artists or paintings. Read the titles and subtitles on each page. Discuss impressionism, post-impressionism, and surrealism. What are the characteristics of each period? Who are the painters associated with each period? Use the suggestions in the TEACHING STRATEGY on TE page 60.

### Presentation and Explanation

❏   Present an oral preview of the information on page 60 before asking students to read the page. Use a worksheet such as the one shown on TE page T45 to encourage reading for information. Guide discussion of the reading. What was different about impressionist art? What were the characteristics of impressionist style? What subjects did impressionist artists choose? Were they successful or not? Why?

❏   Have students read page 61 as a cooperative group activity. Divide the class into four "expert" groups and have each group read and discuss one painter. Then regroup so that each new group contains one member of each "expert" group, who teaches that group's information to the others. Summarize as a whole class, sharing the information from the NOTES CULTURELLES and CONTEXTE HISTORIQUE on TE pages 61 and 62.

❏   Ask students to describe the paintings of Monet shown on pages 62–63; if possible, you could also bring in prints or slides of other Monet paintings. As students read the pages, have them compare their descriptions of Monet's style to the reading. Then have them summarize Monet's life.

❏   Have students present the information on pages 64–65. Divide the class into six groups; have each group read and discuss one painter. Then have them present the information to the rest of the class. Share the information from the TE margin notes, and help students summarize the life, style, and subjects of each artist.

### Guided Practice and Checking Understanding

❏   You may check understanding of these readings by asking students to do a short oral summary of each section. Help other students add information to the summaries.

## Independent Practice

❏ Have students reread the selections independently. Ask them to choose their favorite artist from those presented in the readings and write a short paragraph explaining why that artist is their favorite.

DAY 2

## Motivation and Focus

❏ Begin a project based on the *Interlude culturel*. Have students either choose an interdisciplinary art history project or research one of the artists presented in the text. Use the TEACHING STRATEGIES described on TE pages 60 and 62.

## Presentation and Explanation

❏ Have students read page 66 and the top of 67 to find out characteristics of surrealism. Discuss other paintings they may have seen by Magritte or other surrealist painters. Read the poems on pages 67 and 68 aloud to the students. Have them suggest characteristics of the poems that make them surrealist. Read about the authors and share the information from the TE pages.

❏ Read and discuss the descriptions of the sculptures on page 69. Share the information about the sculptors from the NOTES CULTURELLES on TE page 69. Use the map of Paris on **Overhead Visuals** Transparency 6 to show the location of the sculptures.

## Monitoring and Adjusting

❏ Use the TEACHING STRATEGY: GAME on TE page 68 to monitor students' understanding of the materials in the *Interlude*. If there are answers for which students cannot supply the questions, help them go back through the readings to find those questions.

## Reteaching (as required)

❏ Have students review any sections that they found difficult. Provide background knowledge and vocabulary explanations to help them understand the readings.

## Extension and Enrichment (as desired)

❏ Students may wish to research Cézanne or other French artists of this period who are not described in the readings.
❏ For expansion activities, direct students to www.mcdougallittell.com.

## Summary and Closure

❏ Have students present to the class the results of their interdisciplinary art history projects, or of their research about one of the artists. As they do so, help them summarize what they have learned about French modern art.

## Assessment (optional)

❏ Use **Reading and Culture Tests and Quizzes** for *Interlude culturel 1* to assess students' understanding of the information in this section.

# UNITÉ 2: *Soyons utiles!, Partie 1,* PAGE 70

## BLOCK SCHEDULE (3 DAYS TO COMPLETE)

### Objectives

| | |
|---|---|
| **Communication Functions and Contexts** | To talk about helping around the house |
| | To ask for help and offer help |
| **Linguistic Goals** | To use the subjunctive with *il faut que* to explain what has to be done |
| **Reading and Cultural Objectives** | To understand what the French call *bricolage* |
| | To learn about favorite French pastimes |
| | To understand types of creative activities French young people engage in at home |
| | To read for pleasure |

> ### Block Schedule
>
> **Variety** Ask a student who has a part-time job to go to the board and write the name of their job on the board. The rest of the class then comes up with tasks they think the student's job involves, using the expression **Il faut qu'il/elle**. The student writes each sentence on the board followed by **vrai** or **faux**. When the class has come up with three items that are **vrai**, a new student goes to the board.

### DAY 1

### Motivation and Focus

❏ *Unit Opener:* Look at the photos on pages 70–73, read *Thème et Objectifs* on page 70, and predict the unit's theme. Use the TEACHING STRATEGY, TE page 70, to discuss what the teens are doing in the photo. Compare French and American service opportunities.

### Presentation and Explanation

❏ *Le français pratique (Les travaux domestiques):* Model and have students repeat the expressions in the boxes on pages 74–75. Do the TEACHING STRATEGIES: MULTIPLE INTELLIGENCES, TE page 74, to present and practice the vocabulary.

❏ *Langue et communication (La formation du subjonctif (1)):* Present the formation of the subjunctive, page 78. Explain the use of the subjunctive for expressing necessity and obligation. Model using *il faut que* + subjunctive to talk about personal obligations. Guide students to use the subjunctive to talk about things they need to do.

### Guided Practice and Checking Understanding

❏ Use **Overhead Visuals** Transparency 19 and the overlay, 19(o), with the REVIEW AND PRACTICE activities for *Unité 2* on page A43 to help students practice new vocabulary and the present subjunctive with *il faut*. Use the TEACHING STRATEGY on TE page 76 with the same transparencies to practice talking about chores.

❏ Have students do activities 1-3 (*le français pratique*, pages 115–116) of **Practice Activities** as you play the **Audio**, Cassette 2, Side 1, or read from the **Cassette Script**, pages 8–9.

### Independent Practice

❏ *Pair activities:* Model the activities on pages 75–79. Arrange students in pairs to practice activities 1, 3, and 5 (pages 75–77) and 3, (page 79). Have students check their work using the **Answer Key**. You may do the VARIATION suggestions on TE pages 75 and 76. Ask students to report their partners' responses to the *Et vous?* questions on page 75 to the class.

❏ *Group work:* Students can practice activity 2 (page 79) in groups.

❏ *Homework:* Assign activities 2 and 4 (pages 76–77) and activity 1 (page 79).

## DAY 2

### Motivation and Focus

❑ *Info Magazine:* Have students browse through pages 71–73. Encourage them to write down three interesting points to be shared with the class. Discuss the articles using TEACHING STRATEGIES, TE pages 71–73. Share the NOTES CULTURELLES and NOTES LINGUISTIQUES on TE page 71. Do *Et vous?*, pages 72 and 73.

❑ Students can begin the INTERDISCIPLINARY/COMMUNITY CONNECTIONS services brochure as described on TE page 91.

### Presentation and Explanation

❑ *Langue et communication (Comment exprimer une obligation personnelle: l'usage du subjonctif après **il faut que**):* Explain expressions used for talking about obligations, page 80. Optionally, you may want to present expressions for lack of obligation in *Allons plus loin*, page 80.

❑ *Langue et communication (La formation du subjonctif (2)):* Present verbs with two stems in the subjunctive, page 81. Model the forms in the grammar boxes and have students repeat. Guide students to notice the subject pronouns that use the different stem forms. Explain that the regular subjunctive endings are still used.

### Guided Practice and Checking Understanding

❑ Have students do the *Langue et Communciation* activities on page 116 of **Practice Activities** as you play the Audio, Cassette 2, Side 1, or read from the Cassette Script, page 9.

❑ Review the narrative from **Video** Module 2. Show the Gros plan section of the **Video**, or read from the **Video Script**, and have students do the corresponding activities in the **Video Activity Book**.

### Independent Practice

❑ *Pair Activities:* Model the activities on pages 80–81. Arrange students in pairs to practice activities 6 and 7 (page 81). Have students check their work using the **Answer Key.** You may do the VARIATION suggestion on TE page 80.

❑ *Group work:* Students can practice activity 5 (page 80) in groups.

❑ *Homework:* Assign activity 4 (page 80).

❑ Do the pair crossword puzzle activity in **Teacher to Teacher**, pages 15–17.

### Monitoring and Adjusting

❑ Have students do writing activities 1–5 on pages 27–30 of **Practice Activities**.

❑ As students work on these practice activities, monitor use of the subjunctive and vocabulary for work and household chores. Refer to the vocabulary and grammar boxes on pages 74–81 as needed. Do the TEACHING STRATEGIES, TE pages 74–81, to meet all students' needs.

## DAY 3

### Reteaching (as needed)

❑ Use the *Reference* section of the textbook as needed for reteaching: *Appendix C* page R21 for verbs ending in **-ger**, pages R26–R27 for the irregular verbs **dire**, **lire**, and **écrire**, and pages R24–R30 for **boire**, **prendre**, and **voir**.

❑ Have students do the *Pratique* activity, page 28, in **Practice Activities** to reinforce the verbs **dire**, **lire**, and **écrire**.

## Extension and Enrichment (as desired)

❏ Play the game described on TE page 77 to practice chore vocabulary, and use the TEACHING STRATEGY: EXPANSION suggestion on TE page 79 to have students create their own cartoon situations using the subjunctive.

❏ For expansion activities, direct students to www.mcdougallittell.com.

❏ Have students do the **Block Schedule Activity** at the top of page 15 of these lesson plans.

## Summary and Closure

❏ Show **Overhead Visuals** Transparency 19. Have students suggest what the family members need to do. Then ask students to summarize the vocabulary, language, and communication goals demonstrated.

❏ Revisit *Info Magazine* using the suggestions in the TEACHING STRATEGY in the side margin of TE page 73 and the reading selection on that page. You may want to record students' dialogues for inclusion in their Oral Portfolios. Use the suggestions and forms in **Portfolio Assessment**.

## Assessment

❏ Use the quiz for *Info Magazine* in **Reading and Culture Tests and Quizzes**. Assess understanding of each part of the lesson by administering the **Unit Quiz** for *Partie 1*.

## Notes

# UNITÉ 2: *Soyons utiles!, Partie 2,* PAGE 82

## BLOCK SCHEDULE (4 DAYS TO COMPLETE, INCLUDING UNIT TEST)

### Objectives

**Communication Functions and Contexts**  To ask for help, offer to help, and refuse to help

To describe objects

**Linguistic Goals**  To use subjunctive forms of irregular verbs *être, avoir, aller,* and *faire*

To use the subjunctive after impersonal expressions

To use *vouloir que* and the subjunctive to tell people what you would like them to do

**Reading and Cultural Objectives**  To learn about after-school and summer work of French teens

To read for pleasure and to expand historical knowledge

To read fiction: a medieval fable

> ### Block Schedule
>
> **Process Time** Be sure to practice the formation of the subjunctive before doing the activities. Write some familiar verbs on the board and have students conjugate them in their notebooks. Use regular **-er**, **-ir**, and **-re** verbs like **regarder, choisir, répondre,** etc.

**DAY 1**

### Motivation and Focus

❏  *Info Magazine:* Have students read pages 82–83. Show **Overhead Visuals** Transparencies 20 and 20(o) and have students identify each of the people and discuss how they earn their spending money. Do any or all of the TEACHING STRATEGY activities on TE pages 82 and 83, or *Et vous?* on page 83. Share the NOTE CULTURELLE, TE pages 82–83.

### Presentation and Explanation

❏  *Le français pratique (Pour rendre service):* Model and have students repeat the expressions on page 84 using **Overhead Visuals** Transparency 21 to clarify meanings.

❏  *Langue et communication (Le subjonctif: formation irrégulière):* Present the subjunctive of irregular verbs *être, avoir, aller,* and *faire*, page 86. Use the TEACHING STRATEGY: WARM-UP suggestions on TE page 86 to review uses of the subjunctive.

❏  *Langue et communication (L'usage du subjonctif après certaines expressions impersonnelles):* Explain the use of the subjunctive after impersonal expressions, page 87. Model and have students repeat the expressions in the *Vocabulaire* box. Guide students to give opinions referring to specific people using the subjunctive.

### Guided Practice and Checking Understanding

❏  To check listening comprehension, use the **Audio**, Cassette 2, Side 1, or read **Cassette Script** pages 9–10, as students do activities 1 and 2 (*le français pratique* – page 117) of **Practice Activities**.

### Independent Practice

❏  *Pair activities:* Model the activities on pages 85–87. Students can practice in pairs the *Conversations libres* and activity 1 (page 85), and activities 1–2, 4–5 (pages 86–87). Have students check their work using the **Answer Key**. You may do the VARIATION and EXPANSION suggestions on TE pages 85 and 86.

❏  *Homework:* Assign activity 3 (page 86).

❏  Do any or all of the additional activities in **Teacher to Teacher**, pages 21–29.

## DAY 2

### Monitoring and Adjusting

❏ Do activities 1–4 on pages 31–33 of **Practice Activities**, and *Communication* on page 34.
❏ As students work on the practice activities, monitor use of the subjunctive, expressions for wishes and opinions, and descriptive vocabulary. Refer students back to the boxes on pages 84–91 as needed. Use the TEACHING NOTES, TEACHING STRATEGIES, and NOTES LINGUISTIQUES in the TE margins to help meet all students' needs.

### Presentation and Explanation

❏ *Langue et communication (L'usage du subjonctif après **vouloir que**):* Present this use of the subjunctive, page 88. Do the TEACHING STRATEGY: WARM-UP, TE pages 88–89, to compare the expressions of wish and desire on page 88 with and without **que**.
❏ *Le français pratique (Comment décrire un objet):* Use the TEACHING STRATEGY: WARM-UP, TE page 90, to introduce this optional section. Present the expressions on pages 90–91 with **Overhead Visuals** Transparencies 22 and 22(o). Have students describe classroom objects.

### Guided Practice and Checking Understanding

❏ Use **Overhead Visuals** Transparency 21 with the Goal 1 activity on page A46 to practice talking about wishes and desires. Use Transparency 22 and the suggested activities on page A48 to have students practice describing objects.
❏ To check listening comprehension, use the **Audio,** Cassette 2, Sides 1 and 2, or read **Cassette Script** pages 10-13, as students do activity 3 (*le français pratique* – page 117), *Pratique orale* 1 and 2 (page 118), activities 1-4 (*le français pratique* – pages 118–120) of **Practice Activities**.
❏ Review Module 2 of the **Video**. Play *Problème!* or read from the **Video Script**, and have students do the Problème! and *Supplément* activities in the **Video Activity Book**.

### Independent Practice

❏ *Pair activities:* Model the activities on pages 88–91. Students can practice in pairs activities 6, 8–9 (pages 88–89), and 1–2 (page 91). Have students check their work using the **Answer Key**. You may do the EXPANSION suggestion on TE page 89.
❏ *Homework:* Assign activities 7, 10, and 11 (page 89).
❏ Do any or all of the additional activities in **Teacher to Teacher**, pages 21–29.

## DAY 3

### Reteaching (as needed)

❏ Reteach adjectives with the *Pratique* activity in **Practice Activities**, page 33.

### Extension and Enrichment (as desired)

❏ Do the contest described in the TEACHING STRATEGY on TE page 87 to practice expressing opinions.
❏ If students are interested, have them read the fable, *Lecture: La couverture*, pages 93–96.
❏ For expansion activities, direct students to www.mcdougallittell.com.
❏ Have students do the **Block Schedule Activity** at the top of page 18 of these lesson plans.

## Summary and Closure

❑ Show **Overhead Visuals** Transparencies 20 and 20(o). Students can choose one of the people in the picture, describe the person's job, and give their opinion of the job, as suggested in the Goal 1 activity, page A44. Other students can summarize the goals of the lesson.

❑ *Lecture (La couverture):* Introduce the reading with the TEACHING STRATEGY, TE page 92, and *Avant de lire,* page 92. Use *Anticipons un peu!,* page 92, and **Overhead Visuals** Transparency L2 to help students make predictions about the fable. Have students read the story in pairs, answering all *Avez-vous compris?* questions and doing *Anticipons un peu!.* Share the NOTES CULTURELLES and NOTES LINGUISTIQUES, TE pages 92–97. Use the quiz for *Lecture* in **Reading and Culture Tests and Quizzes**. Have pairs of students prepare the role plays on page 97, using **Overhead Visuals** Transparency L2 for cues.

❑ Do any of the *Après la lecture* activities on page 97. These activities may be included in students' Written or Oral Portfolios; see STUDENT PORTFOLIOS suggestions, TE page 97.

## Assessment

❑ Use the quiz for *Info Magazine* in **Reading and Culture Tests and Quizzes**. Assess understanding of each part of the lesson by administering the **Unit Quiz** for *Partie 2.*

## Reteaching (as needed)

❑ Redo any of the activities in **Practice Activities** that caused students difficulty.

## Assessment

❑ Administer **Unit Test 2** after completing the unit. Give any or all of the **Proficiency Tests** for the unit: **Listening Comprehension Performance**, **Speaking Performance**, and **Writing Performance**.

## Notes

# INTERLUDE CULTUREL 2: *Les grands moments de l'histoire de France (jusqu'en 1453),* PAGE 98

## BLOCK SCHEDULE (2 DAYS TO COMPLETE – OPTIONAL)

### Objectives

**Reading Objectives**   To read for content: information about early French history

To read an ***Astérix*** cartoon

To read about *La Chanson de Roland*

**Cultural Objectives**   To learn about important periods and events of early French history

To learn about important leaders: Vercingétorix, Charlemagne, Roland, Guillaume le Conquérant, Aliénor d'Aquitaine, Jeanne d'Arc

To learn about literature related to early French history: ***Astérix***, *La Chanson de Roland*

**Note:** The *Interlude culturel* contains cultural information about French history. It can be taught as a lesson or introduced in smaller sections as parts of other lessons. The material in this section can be used to expand cultural awareness, as source material for student research projects, to develop reading skills, or to build cultural knowledge.

### DAY 1

### Motivation and Focus

❏   Have students preview the pictures on pages 98–107, inviting them to share information they may remember about ***Astérix*** or Joan of Arc. If possible, show portions of a film on Joan of Arc. Read the titles and subtitles on each page. Discuss the historical periods on the time line, page 98. What are the different periods? What are the dates of these periods? Which people are important in each of these times? Use the suggestions in the TEACHING STRATEGY on TE page 98.

### Presentation and Explanation

❏   Preview the information on page 98 with **Overhead Visuals** Transparencies H1, 5 and 5(o), and 1 and 1(o). Students can read and discuss the page. What were the important events of each of the periods? What area(s) of Europe and France were involved? Have students read page 99 in cooperative groups. Divide into three groups, with each group reading about a different hero. After reading, invite groups to share information about their hero: Who was he or she? When did the person live? What did the person do for France?

❏   Ask students to read the text and ***Astérix*** cartoon on pages 100–101. As students read the pages, have them refer back to the time line on page 98 to find the dates for the fictional character. Then have them summarize the cartoon and describe the characteristics of ***Astérix*** that make him so popular. Share the NOTES LINGUISTIQUES and NOTES CULTURELLES on TE pages 100–101.

❏   Have students read pages 102–103 to become familiar with historical and legendary facts about Roland. Share the information in the TE margin notes. Students can discuss what they have found out about Roland. As a class, compare Roland to an American historical hero whose actions have also become legendary.

### Guided Practice and Checking Understanding

❏   You may check understanding of these readings by asking students to do a short oral summary of each section. Help other students add information to the summaries.

## Motivation and Focus

❏   Begin a project based on the *Interlude culturel.* Have students choose either an interdisciplinary history or literature project, or research one of the people presented in the text.

## Presentation and Explanation

❏   Have students read pages 104–105 to find out about French influence in England, explaining that students do not need to remember all of the names in the selection. Guide students to summarize the information using the maps on pages 104–105 or **Overhead Visuals** Transparencies 1 and 5 (with overlays) to point out important places. Discuss the Bayeux Tapestry, sharing the NOTE CULTURELLE, TE page 104.

❏   Use the pictures and captions on pages 106–107 to preview the life of Joan of Arc. Read and discuss the selection. Share the information from the NOTES CULTURELLES and NOTE HISTORIQUE on TE pages 106–107. Use the map of France on **Overhead Visuals** Transparency 1 and 1(o) to show the sites mentioned in the selection.

## Independent Practice

❏   Have students reread the selections independently. Ask them to choose their favorite French hero from those presented in the readings and write a short paragraph explaining why that person is their favorite.

## Monitoring and Adjusting

❏   Use the TEACHING STRATEGY: GAME on TE page 107 to monitor students' understanding of the material in the *Interlude.* If there are answers for which students cannot supply the questions, help them go back through the readings to find those questions.

## Reteaching (as required)

❏   Have students review any sections that they found difficult. Provide background knowledge and vocabulary explanations to help them understand the readings.

## Extension and Enrichment (as desired)

❏   Students may wish to research medieval castles or Roman archaeological sites in France.
❏   For expansion activities, direct students to www.mcdougallittell.com.

## Summary and Closure

❏   Have students present to the class the results of their interdisciplinary history projects, or of their research about one of the French heros. As they do so, help them summarize what they have learned about French history.

## Assessment (optional)

❏   Use **Reading and Culture Tests and Quizzes** for *Interlude culturel 2* to assess students' understanding of the information in this section.

# UNITÉ 3: *Vive la nature, Partie 1,* PAGE 108

## BLOCK SCHEDULE (3 DAYS TO COMPLETE)

### Objectives

| | |
|---|---|
| **Communication Functions and Contexts** | To talk about outdoor activities |
| | To talk about vacation pleasures and problems |
| | To describe the natural environment and how to protect it |
| **Linguistic Goals** | To use the *passé composé* to talk about the past |
| | To use the *imparfait* and *passé composé* to narrate past events |
| **Reading and Cultural Objectives** | To understand why the French people feel close to their roots |
| | To understand how the French people feel about their environment |
| | To understand how the French incorporate *tourisme écologique* into their vacation plans |
| | To read for pleasure and to scan for information |

> **Block Schedule**
>
> **Change of Pace** In small groups, have students describe a real or imaginary Earth Day in which they participated. They should write 6-8 sentences describing the environmentally friendly activities they did during the day. Tell them to use both the *imparfait* and the *passé composé* in their writing. One student from each group can read the group's work aloud when finished.

### DAY 1

### Motivation and Focus

❏ *Unit Opener:* Discuss the photos on pages 108–111 and have students guess the unit's topic. Read *Thème et Objectifs* on page 108 and discuss the importance of nature and the environment. How do French and American teenagers enjoy and protect nature?

❏ *Info Magazine:* Have students work in pairs or small groups to read through any or all of the articles on pages 109–111, looking for cultural similarities or differences between French and American views toward environment and nature. See the TEACHING STRATEGY on TE page 109. Students can share their discoveries with the class. Share the NOTES CULTURELLES and NOTES LINGUISTIQUES on TE pages 109 and 110. Use the TEACHING STRATEGY, TE page 110, with the *Et vous?* activity on textbook page 110. Have students do *Et vous?*, page 111.

### Presentation and Explanation

❏ *Le français pratique (Les vacances: Plaisirs et problèmes):* Present the vocabulary on page 112 with **Overhead Visuals** Transparencies 23 and 24. Model and have students repeat. Help students talk about favorite vacation activities and possible dangers.

❏ *Langue et communication (Revision: Le passé composé):* Review forms of the *passé composé*, page 114, as needed. Explain the use of *avoir* and *être* as auxiliary verbs, and agreement between past participle and subjects with verbs that use *être*. Model expressions with adverbs and have students repeat, guiding them to understand the position of adverbs in the sentences. Optionally, explain the meaning differences for verbs that are conjugated with *être* or *avoir* in *Allons plus loin,* page 114.

### Guided Practice and Checking Understanding

❏ Use **Overhead Visuals** Transparencies 23 and 24 and the activities on pages A50–A51 to help students practice talking about vacation activities and problems.

❏ Have students do activities 1–4 (*le français pratique* – pages 121–122) of **Practice Activities** as you play the **Audio**, Cassette 3, Side 1, or read from the **Cassette Script**, pages 14–15.

## Independent Practice

❑ *Pair activities:* Model the activities on pages 113–115. Do activity 1 and *Conversations libres* (page 113), and activities 1–2 (pages 114–115) in pairs. Students can check their answers in the **Answer Key**. Do the EXPANSION suggestion, TE page 113.
❑ *Homework:* Assign activities 3–4 (page 115).
❑ Do the activities in **Teacher to Teacher**, pages 33–36.

### DAY 2

## Motivation and Focus

❑ Begin the INTERDISCIPLINARY/COMMUNITY CONNECTIONS project, TE page 133. Students will work in groups to prepare a travel brochure or video in French.

## Presentation and Explanation

❑ *Langue et communication (Revision: L'imparfait):* Review the imperfect with the TEACHING STRATEGY: WARM-UP, TE page 116. Explain its use for what used to be or what was happening in the past. Review imperfect stem formation and the irregular stem for *être*. Remind students of forms for *-ger* and *-cer* verbs.
❑ *Langue et communication (L'usage du passé composé et de l'imparfait):* Compare the use of the **passé composé** and **imparfait**, page 118. Model the examples and guide students to explain the difference in meanings of the tenses. Explain the NOTE LINGUISTIQUE, TE page 118.

## Guided Practice and Checking Understanding

❑ Have students do *Pratique orale* 1–3 (*langue et communication* – page 123) of **Practice Activities** as you play the **Audio**, Cassette 3, Side 1, or read from the **Cassette Script**, page 16.
❑ Show **Video** Module 3, or read the **Video Script**, and have students do the Mise en scène and Gros plan activities in the **Video Activity Book**.

## Independent Practice

❑ *Pair activities:* Model the activities on pages 116–119. Do activities 5–7, 9, and 11 (pages 116–118) in pairs. Students can check their answers in the **Answer Key**. Do the EXPANSION suggestion, TE page 117.
❑ *Group work:* Students can practice activities 8 (page 117) and 14 (page 119) in groups.
❑ *Homework:* Assign activities 10, and 12–13 (pages 118 and 119).

## Monitoring and Adjusting

❑ Have students do writing activities 1–4 on pages 35–38 of **Practice Activities**.
❑ During the practice activities, monitor use of the **passé composé** and imperfect tenses and vocabulary. Refer to the boxes on pages 112–118 as needed. Do the TEACHING STRATEGIES on TE pages 114–118 to meet all students' needs.

### DAY 3

## Reteaching (as needed)

❑ Reteach verbs and tenses using the *Reference* section of the textbook as needed: *Appendix C* pages R20–R23 for verbs like **jeter** and **détruire**, and *Appendix A* pages R4 and *Appendix C* pages R22–R31 for irregular past participles and verbs conjugated with **être**.

❏ Redo any of the activities in **Practice Activities** with which students had difficulty.

## Extension and Enrichment (as desired)

❏ Students can create environmental posters with the TEACHING STRATEGY: INTERDISCIPLINARY/COMMUNITY CONNECTIONS activity on TE page 111.
❏ Play the game described on TE page 112 to practice vacation vocabulary.
❏ For expansion activities, direct students to www.mcdougallittell.com.
❏ If students are interested, they can read portions of *Interlude culturel 3*, pages 140–147.
❏ Have students do the **Block Schedule Activity** at the top of page 23 of these lesson plans.

## Summary and Closure

❏ Use **Overhead Visuals** Transparency 24. Ask students to develop and present a narration in the past based on one of the photos. Guide other students to summarize the communicative, linguistic, and cultural goals demonstrated.
❏ Use the STUDENT PORTFOLIOS suggestions on TE pages 115 and 119.

## Assessment

❏ Use the quiz for *Info Magazine* in **Reading and Culture Tests and Quizzes**. Administer the **Unit Quiz** for *Partie 1* to assess understanding.

## Notes

# UNITÉ 3: *Vive la nature, Partie 2,* PAGE 120

## BLOCK SCHEDULE (4 DAYS TO COMPLETE, INCLUDING UNIT TEST)

## Objectives

| | |
|---|---|
| **Communication Functions and Contexts** | To talk about weather conditions and natural phenomena |
| | To describe habitual past actions |
| | To narrate a sequence of past events |
| **Linguistic Goals** | To use the **passé composé** and **imparfait** to narrate past events |
| | To recognize the **passé simple** in written narration and literary texts |
| **Reading and Cultural Objectives** | To learn why the Cousteau family is so well-known and what important work they do |
| | To understand what the **culte du soleil** represents for French people |
| | To read for pleasure |
| | To read fiction: a short story by Goscinny, illustrated by Sempé |

> ### Block Schedule
>
> **Variety** Have students bring a picture of a favorite event that they remember well. Have them share the picture and memories with others in small groups. Students should use both the *imparfait* and the *passé composé* in their descriptions.

### DAY 1

## Motivation and Focus

❑ *Info Magazine:* Preview the photos on pages 120–123 and discuss how they are connected to ecology. Use the TEACHING STRATEGY, TE page 120, to guide students as they read about Jacques Cousteau. Ask students to read page 121. Discuss ways to preserve the environment, using the TEACHING STRATEGY on TE page 121. Read pages 122–123 and do the TEACHING STRATEGY activities or *Et vous?* on TE page 123. Explain the NOTES CULTURELLES, TE page 122. Read the poem on page 123 aloud as students follow in their books. Discuss imagery of the sun in the poem.

❑ You may want to have students begin a research project as described in INTERDISCIPLINARY/COMMUNITY CONNECTIONS PROJECT on TE page 122.

## Presentation and Explanation

❑ *Le français pratique (Quoi de neuf?):* Model and have students repeat the expressions and vocabulary for describing events on pages 124–125. Help students use the expressions to talk about recent events at school or in the local area.

❑ *Le français pratique (Comment parler de la pluie et du beau temps):* Use **Overhead Visuals** Transparency 25 to introduce weather expressions as described in the TEACHING STRATEGY, TE page 126. Students can discuss the weather or make their own weather predictions using the vocabulary on page 126.

## Guided Practice and Checking Understanding

❑ Use **Overhead Visuals** Transparency 25 with the activities on pages A53–A54 to practice talking about weather conditions.

❑ Check listening comprehension with the **Audio**, Cassette 3, Side 2, or read **Cassette Script** pages 16–19, as students do activities 1–5 (*le français pratique* – pages 124–126) of **Practice Activities**.

## Independent Practice

❑ *Pair activities:* Model the activities on pages 125–127. Do activities 2–3 and *Conversations libres* (pages 125 and 127) in pairs. Have students check their work in the **Answer Key**.

❏ Do any of the activities on **Teacher to Teacher** pages 32–34.

## DAY 2

### Presentation and Explanation

❏ *Langue et communication (La description d'un événement: le passé composé et l'imparfait; L'imparfait et le passé composé dans la même phrase):* Use the TEACHING STRATEGY, TE pages 128–129, to compare the **passé composé** and imperfect tenses. Have students study the chart on page 128. Explain how the two tenses can be used in the same sentence, page 131. Model the examples, guide students to identify the verb tenses in each clause, and explain their uses. Model and have students repeat the time expressions on page 131.

❏ *Langue et communication (Le passé simple):* Introduce the use of the **passé simple** to describe what happened in written narration, page 133. Model the examples and guide students to discover the pattern for forming the stem and the endings.

### Guided Practice and Checking Understanding

❏ Review **Video** Module 3. Show *Problème!*, or read from the **Video Script**, and have students do the *Problème!* and *Supplément* activities in the **Video Activity Book**.

### Independent Practice

❏ *Pair activities:* Model the activities on pages 128–133. Do activities 1, 3, 5, 6, 7, 10, and 11 (pages 128–133) in pairs. Have students check their work in the **Answer Key**. Do the VARIATIONS on TE page 129.

❏ *Homework:* Assign activities 2 (page 129), 4 (page 130), and 8 and 9 (page 132).

❏ Do any of the activities on **Teacher to Teacher** pages 37–46.

### Monitoring and Adjusting

❏ Have students do the writing activities on pages 39–44 of **Practice Activities**.

❏ Monitor expressions for weather and events and use of the **passé composé**, imperfect, and **passé simple** as students work on the practice activities. Refer students to the boxes on pages 124–133 as needed. Use the TEACHING STRATEGIES and EXPANSION suggestions in the TE margins to meet all students' needs.

## DAY 3

### Reteaching (as needed)

❏ Reteach the **passé simple** and compare to other past tenses on *Appendix C* pages R32–R33.

### Extension and Enrichment (as desired)

❏ Students can read the short story in *Lecture: King,* pages 135–138, or choose one of the *Interlude culturel 3* selections on pages 140–147 for enrichment reading.

❏ For expansion activities, direct students to www.mcdougallittell.com.

❏ Have students do the **Block Schedule Activity** at the top of page 26 of these lesson plans.

### Summary and Closure

❏ Show **Overhead Visuals** Transparencies 26 and 27 and ask students to describe what they saw or what happened to them, using the Goal 1 activities on pages A56 and A58. Have others summarize the communicative and linguistic goals demonstrated.

❏ *Lecture (King):* Read and discuss *Avant de lire* and *Note culturelle,* page 134. Use *Anticipons un peu!* to help students make predictions about the story. Students can read the story, pages 135–138, answering *Avez-vous compris?* questions and doing *Anticipons un peu!* throughout. Use the TEACHING STRATEGIES on TE pages 137 and 138. Use the quiz for *Lecture* in **Reading and Culture Tests and Quizzes.** Use **Overhead Visuals** Transparency L3 as students role play the *Situations* on page 139.

❏ Do any of the STUDENT PORTFOLIOS suggestions on TE pages 123 and 139.

## Assessment

❏ Use the quiz for *Info Magazine* in **Reading and Culture Tests and Quizzes.** Assess understanding of *Partie 2* by administering the appropriate **Unit Quiz.**

## Reteaching (as needed)

❏ Use the TEACHING STRATEGY, TE page 130, to review use of the *passé composé* and *imparfait* in describing past events.

## Assessment

❏ Administer **Unit Test 3** after completing the unit. Use any or all of the **Proficiency Tests** for the unit: **Listening Comprehension Performance, Speaking Performance,** and **Writing Performance.**

## Notes

# INTERLUDE CULTUREL 3: *Les grands moments de l'histoire de France (1453–1715)*, PAGE 140

## BLOCK SCHEDULE (2 DAYS TO COMPLETE – OPTIONAL)

### Objectives

**Reading Objectives**  To read for content: information about the classical period of French history

To read a summary of *Cyrano de Bergerac*

To read a fable: *Le corbeau et le renard* by Jean de La Fontaine

**Cultural Objectives**  To learn about *La Renaissance* and *Le Grand Siècle* in French history

To learn about François I$^{er}$, Léonard de Vinci, Louis XIV, Cyrano de Bergerac

To learn about French **châteaux** and architectural styles

**Note:** The *Interlude culturel* contains information about the classical period of French history. It can be taught as a lesson or introduced in smaller sections as parts of other lessons. The reading selections can be used to expand cultural awareness, as a source for student research projects, to develop reading skills, or to build cultural knowledge.

### DAY 1

### Motivation and Focus

❏  As students preview the pictures on pages 140–147, encourage comments about the people and events, clothing, and architecture. Together, read the titles and subtitles on each of the pages. If possible, show sections of the movie version of *Cyrano* as described in the TEACHING STRATEGY, TE page 140.

### Presentation and Explanation

❏  Use **Overhead Visuals** Transparencies H2, 1, and 1(o) to present orally the information about *La Renaissance* and *Le Grand Siècle* on pages 140–141. Have students read and discuss the pages. What happened in France during these times? Who were the important people of these times? Students can read pages 140–141 in groups. Divide the class into four groups with each group reading about a time period or important person. After reading, invite groups to share information about their section. Explain the NOTES HISTORIQUES and NOTES CULTURELLES on TE page 141.

❏  Ask students to read pages 142–145 to learn about the real Cyrano de Bergerac and the character in literature and movies. If possible, use portions of the Rappeneau movie in class as described in the TEACHING NOTE, TE page 142. See the suggestions for using movies on TE pages T50–T51. Students can discuss the movie poster using the TEACHING STRATEGY, TE page 142. Share the NOTES CULTURELLES and NOTES LINGUISTIQUES in the TE margins. Use the TEACHING STRATEGY, TE page 145, to have students discuss the ending and propose alternative endings for the movie.

### Guided Practice and Checking Understanding

❏  You may check understanding of the readings by asking students to do a short oral summary of each section. Help other students add information to the summaries.

### Monitoring and Adjusting

❏  Use the TEACHING STRATEGY, TE page 144, to have students retell the story of Cyrano de Bergerac. If students have difficulty, help them go back through the selection to find the correct captions and order for the story.

## DAY 2

### Motivation and Focus

❏ Begin a project based on the *Interlude culturel*. Students can research one of the people, time periods, or castles presented in the text.

### Presentation and Explanation

❏ Read together the introduction to *Le corbeau et le renard* on page 146. Students can read and discuss the fable and compare it to other fables they know. Explain the NOTES LINGUISTIQUES in the TE margin. Use the TEACHING STRATEGY on TE page 146 to guide a discussion of the fable's moral.

❏ Present an overview of the **châteaux** on page 147, using **Overhead Visuals** Transparencies 1 and 1(o) to help students find the locations of the castles. Students can describe the various castles in the photos and talk about which one they like best. Ask students to read page 147 and share an interesting fact about their favorite castle. Explain the NOTES CULTURELLES and ANECDOTE on TE page 147.

### Independent Practice

❏ Students can reread the selections independently. Ask them to choose their favorite castle or person from those presented in the readings and write a short paragraph explaining why it is their favorite.

### Reteaching (as required)

❏ Have students review any sections that they found difficult. Provide background knowledge and vocabulary explanations to help them understand the readings.

### Extension and Enrichment (as desired)

❏ Students may wish to research other castles or find out about other fables by La Fontaine to share with the class.
❏ For expansion activities, direct students to www.mcdougallittell.com.

### Summary and Closure

❏ Students can present to the class their project results about the people, time periods, and castles. As students make their presentations, help the class summarize what they have learned about French history.

### Assessment (optional)

❏ Use **Reading and Culture Tests and Quizzes** for *Interlude culturel 3* to assess students' understanding of the information in this section.

# UNITÉ 4: *Aspects de la vie quotidienne, Partie 1,* PAGE 148

## BLOCK SCHEDULE (3 DAYS TO COMPLETE)

## Objectives

| | |
|---|---|
| **Communication Functions and Contexts** | To be able to buy stamps and mail letters |
| | To be able to purchase small items you might need |
| **Linguistic Goals** | To use object pronouns **y** and *en* |
| | To use indefinite expressions of quantity |
| **Reading and Cultural Objectives** | To learn about where to buy various items and obtain services in France |
| | To compare and contrast French and American shopping habits |
| | To read for pleasure |

### Block Schedule

**Fun Break** In pairs, have students play the roles of a store owner and a customer. Students should develop a short dialogue in which they ask for and purchase some things in a store. Allow volunteers to present their dialogues to the class.

### DAY 1

## Motivation and Focus

❏   *Unit Opener:* Ask students to look through the photos and pictures on pages 148–151 and identify the different shops, stores, and daily activities that are represented. Read together *Thème et Objectifs* to preview the content of the unit. Students can talk about their own daily life activities and the places they go for services.

❏   *Info Magazine:* Ask students to browse through pages 149–151. Remind them to use cognates and guess meaning from context. Students can share interesting information they found about French shopping habits and compare them to American habits. Explain the PHOTO NOTES, NOTES LINGUISTIQUES, and NOTES CULTURELLES in the TE margins. Use any or all of the TEACHING STRATEGIES, TE pages 150–151, or do *Et vous?,* page 150.

## Presentation and Explanation

❏   *Le français pratique (Comment faire des achats):* Model the expressions and vocabulary on pages 152–153 for students to repeat. Use **Overhead Visuals** Transparencies 28–31 to clarify meanings. Explain the NOTES LINGUISTIQUES in the TE margins and use the TEACHING STRATEGY, TE page 153, to help students practice the vocabulary.

## Guided Practice and Checking Understanding

❏   Use **Overhead Visuals** Transparencies 28–31 and the activities on pages A60–A65 to help students practice new vocabulary and shopping dialogues in various stores. Students can practice talking about where to buy items using Transparency 32 and the Goal 1 activity on page A67.

❏   Have students do activities 1–4 (*le français pratique* – pages 127–128) of **Practice Activities** as you play the **Audio,** Cassette 4, Side 1, or read from the **Cassette Script,** pages 20–22.

❏   Use the TEACHING STRATEGY: WARM-UP on TE pages 154–155 to have students practice dialogues about making purchases.

## Independent Practice

❏   *Pair activities:* Model the activities on pages 154–155. Arrange students in pairs to practice activities 1, 4–5, and *Conversations libres* (pages 154–155). Have students check their work in the **Answer Key.**

❏   *Homework:* Assign activities 2 and 3 on page 154. You may want to do the VARIATION (TE page 154) suggestion for Activity 3.

### DAY 2

## Motivation and Focus

❑ Students can work in groups to begin planning a local services directory as described in INTERDISCIPLINARY/COMMUNITY CONNECTIONS on TE page 169.

## Presentation and Explanation

❑ *Langue et communication (Révision: le pronom y; Révision: le pronom en)*: Review the object pronouns *y* and *en*, page 156. Model the examples for students to repeat. Remind students of the meanings and placement of the object pronouns within sentences. Explain the NOTES LINGUISTIQUES, TE page 156. Use the *Rappel!* box to review exceptions in placement of the pronouns.
❑ *Langue et communication (Expressions indéfinies de quantité):* Present the expressions for indefinite quantities on page 158. Explain their use as adjectives and pronouns and as subjects and objects of the verb. Model the examples and have students repeat.

## Guided Practice and Checking Understanding

❑ Have students do the *Langue et Communication* activities on page 129 of **Practice Activities** as you play the **Audio**, Cassette 4, Side 1, or read from the Cassette Script, pages 21-22.
❑ Show **Video** Module 4 Mise en scène and Gros plan, and have students do the corresponding activities in the **Video Activity Book**.

## Independent Practice

❑ *Pair Activities:* Model the activities on pages 157—159. Arrange students in pairs to practice activities 1-5 (page 157—159). Have students check their work using the **Answer Key**. You may do the TEACHING NOTE suggestion on TE page 157.
❑ Do any of the activities in **Teacher to Teacher**, pages 50—53.

## Monitoring and Adjusting

❑ Have students do writing activities 1—5 on pages 45—48 of **Practice Activities**.
❑ Monitor use of vocabulary, object pronouns, and indefinite quantity expressions as students work on the practice activities. Refer to the boxes on pages 152—153, 156, and 158 as needed. Do the TEACHING NOTE (TE page 152) and TEACHING STRATEGIES (TE pages 156 and 158) to meet all students' needs.

### DAY 3

## Reteaching (as needed)

❑ Play the game in TEACHING STRATEGY, TE page 157, to reteach object pronouns *y* and *en*.
❑ Use the *Rappel!* box, page 156, to review placement of the pronouns *y* and *en* in affirmative commands.

## Extension and Enrichment (as desired)

❑ Use the NOTES CULTURELLES on TE pages 152—153 and 159 to share information about the French postal system and Montreal. Introduce SUPPLEMENTARY VOCABULARY and explain ADDITIONAL INFORMATION notes, TE pages 152—153 and 155.
❑ For expansion activities, direct students to www.mcdougallittell.com.
❑ Students may want to choose one of the selections in *Interlude culturel 4*, pages 176—185, to read about French music and musicians.
❑ Have students do the **Block Schedule Activity** at the top of page 31 of these lesson plans.

## Summary and Closure

❑ Show **Overhead Visuals** Transparency 28, 29, 30, 31, or 32 and ask students to do the corresponding Goal 1 activities on page A60, A62, A63, A65, or A67. Guide students to summarize the communicative, linguistic, and cultural goals demonstrated.

❑ You may want to record one of the *Conversations libres*, page 154, to include in students' Oral Portfolios.

## Assessment

❑ Use the quiz for *Info Magazine* in **Reading and Culture Tests and Quizzes**. Assess understanding by giving the **Unit Quiz** for *Partie 1*.

## Notes

# UNITÉ 4: *Aspects de la vie quotidienne, Partie 2,* PAGE 160

## BLOCK SCHEDULE (4 DAYS TO COMPLETE, INCLUDING UNIT TEST)

### Objectives

**Communication Functions and Contexts**
To be able to have items fixed or cleaned
To be able to get a haircut
To be able to ask for a variety of services

**Linguistic Goals**
To answer questions and refer to people, things, and places using object pronouns
To use *faire* + infinitive to describe actions that people have others do for them

**Reading and Cultural Objectives**
To learn where to obtain various services
To read for pleasure
To read a humorous play: *Une histoire de cheveux*

### Block Schedule

**Peer Teaching** Have students choose a concept with which they are struggling. Divide the class into groups. Have students brainstorm for 5 minutes to come up with suggestions for an easy way to remember the concept. Have groups share ideas with the class.

### DAY 1

### Motivation and Focus

❏   *Info Magazine:* Have students comment on the hairstyles pictured on page 160. Read the introduction and use the TEACHING STRATEGY at the bottom of TE page 160 to have students talk about styles. Use the TEACHING NOTE and NOTE LINGUISTIQUE in the TE margin to review and explain vocabulary.

### Presentation and Explanation

❏   *Le français pratique (Au salon de coiffure):* Show **Overhead Visuals** Transparency 33 as you present the hairdressing vocabulary and expressions on page 161. Model the expressions and have students repeat.

❏   *Langue et communication (Révision: les pronoms le, la, les and lui, leur; L'ordre des pronoms):* Review object pronouns, page 162. Follow the TEACHING NOTES in the TE margin. Present the usual order of object pronouns, page 164. Guide students to discover the different order used in affirmative commands. Model the examples for students to repeat. Optionally, you may want to explain the NOTE LINGUISTIQUE, TE page 164, and the order of pronouns with reflexive verbs in *Allons plus loin,* page 164.

### Guided Practice and Checking Understanding

❏   Use **Overhead Visuals** Transparency 33 with the Goal 1 activities on page A69 to practice explaining services desired from a hairdresser.

❏   To check listening, use the **Audio**, Cassette 4, Side 1, or read from **Cassette Script** pages 22–24 as students do Activities 1–3 (*le français pratique* – page 130) and *Pratique Orale* 1 and 2 (*langue et communcation* – page 131) of **Practice Activities**.

### Independent Practice

❏   *Pair activities:* Model the activities on pages 161–165. Students can practice these activities in pairs: 1 (page 161) and 1–8 (pages 163–165). Have students check their work with the **Answer Key**. Use the EXPANSION and PERSONALIZATION suggestions on TE page 163.

### DAY 2

## Presentation and Explanation

❏  *Le français pratique (Services):* Present expressions for asking for services, page 166. Demonstrate meanings with **Overhead Visuals** Transparencies 34 and 35 or the Teaching Strategy, TE page 166. Explain the Notes linguistiques.

❏  *Langue et communication (La construction **faire** + infinitif):* Explain the use of **faire** + infinitive, page 168. Model the examples and have students repeat. You may want to introduce the use of **faire** + infinitive in specific expressions and in describing actions that people are having done for themselves in *Allons plus loin*, page 168.

## Guided Practice and Checking Understanding

❏  Use Transparencies 34 and 35 with the suggested activities on pages A70–A73 to have students practice asking about services in other types of stores and repair shops.

❏  Review **Video** Module 4. Show the *Problème!* section and do the *Problème!* and *Supplément* activities in the **Video Activity Book**. Show Module 5 Mise en scène and do the corresponding activities.

❏  To check listening, use the **Audio**, Cassette 4, Side 2, or read from **Cassette Script** pages 24–26 as students do **Activities** 1–3 (*le français pratique* – pages 131–132) and the Pratique orale (*langue et communication* – page 132) of Practice Activities.

## Independent Practice

❏  *Pair activities:* Model the activities on pages 167–169. Students can practice these activities in pairs: 1–2 (page 167), and 1–2 (page 169). Have students check their work with the **Answer Key**.

❏  Choose any of the additional activities in **Teacher to Teacher**, pages 47–49 and 54–57.

## Monitoring and Adjusting

❏  Check students' responses as they do writing activities 1–3 on pages 49–51, activity 1 on page 52, and the Communication activities on pages 53–54 of **Practice Activities**.

❏  Monitor use of object pronouns, **faire** + infinitive, and vocabulary as students work on the practice activities. Refer students back to the boxes on pages 161–168 as needed. Use the Teaching Strategies on TE pages 164 and 168 to meet all students' needs.

### DAY 3

## Reteaching (as needed)

❏  Use the Pratique activities on pages 49 and 51–52 of **Practice Activities** to reteach past participle agreement with object pronouns and **faire** + infinitive expressions.

## Extension and Enrichment (as desired)

❏  Practice pronouns by playing the game in the Teaching Strategy on TE page 162.

❏  Share the information about Switzerland and Lac Léman in the Notes culturelles, TE page 163. Students can find out more information to share with the class.

❏  For expansion activities, direct students to www.mcdougallittell.com.

❏  Have students read *Une histoire de cheveux* on pages 171–174, or one of the *Interlude culturel 4* selections on pages 176–185, for enjoyment.

❑ Have students do the **Block Schedule Activity** at the top of page 34 of these lesson plans.

## Summary and Closure

❑ Show **Overhead Visuals** Transparency 34 and invite pairs to choose one of the photos and create a conversation as described in the Goal 1 activity on page A71. Have other students summarize the communicative and linguistic goals demonstrated.

❑ *Lecture (Une histoire de cheveux):* Use the *Avant de lire* activity on page 170 to preview the text as suggested in the TEACHING STRATEGY, TE page 170. Have students read the comedy on pages 171–174, stopping to answer the *Avez-vous compris?* questions and do the *Anticipons un peu!*. Share the information on TE pages 170–173, as appropriate: REALIA NOTES, NOTES LINGUISTIQUES, and TEACHING STRATEGIES. Students can summarize the story using **Overhead Visuals** Transparency L4 as an aid. Use the quiz for *Lecture* in **Reading and Culture Tests and Quizzes**. Choose any of the oral or written *Après la lecture* activities on page 175 as a culminating activity.

❑ Use the STUDENT PORTFOLIOS suggestions on TE pages 167 and 175, or the oral EXPANSION: ACTIVITY 2 on TE page 169, for students' Written or Oral Portfolios.

## Assessment

❑ Use the quiz for *Info Magazine* in **Reading and Culture Tests and Quizzes** and the corresponding **Unit Quiz** to assess understanding of *Partie 2*.

### DAY 4

## Reteaching (as needed)

❑ Redo any of the activities in **Practice Activities** that caused students difficulty.

## Assessment

❑ After completing the unit's activities, have students do **Unit Test 4**. In addition, you may want to choose any or all of the **Proficiency Tests** for the unit: **Listening Comprehension Performance, Speaking Performance**, and **Writing Performance**.

## Notes

# INTERLUDE CULTUREL 4: *Vive la musique!*, PAGE 176

## BLOCK SCHEDULE (2 DAYS TO COMPLETE – OPTIONAL)

### Objectives

**Reading Objectives**    To read for content: information about the musical landscape of France and the French-speaking world

To read a song: *Mon pays* by Vigneault

**Cultural Objectives**    To learn about famous French singers of yesterday and today: Édith Piaf, Joséphine Baker, and contemporary stars

To learn about the multi-cultural aspect of music from the francophone world

To learn about French classical musicians: Lully, Chopin, Bizet, and Debussy

**Note:** This *Interlude culturel* gives an overview of music from medieval through contemporary times. It can be taught as a lesson or read in smaller sections as parts of other lessons. Use the material to meet the needs and interests of the class: to expand cultural awareness, as source material for students research projects, to develop reading skills, or to build cultural knowledge.

---

### DAY 1

### Motivation and Focus

❏   Ask students to name French singers and musicians; list the names on the board. If possible, bring in recordings of French songs for students to listen to as they look through the *Interlude* on pages 176–185, as suggested in the TEACHING STRATEGY on TE page 176. Have students add other names or music that they recognize from the *Interlude*. Guide discussion of the photos. Who are these musicians? What kind of music do you think they perform? Use **Overhead Visuals** Transparencies H1–H4 to help students understand where the musical periods are in relation to other events in history.

### Presentation and Explanation

❏   Present an oral preview of the information on pages 176–177. Have students read for information, looking for information about the people and time periods pictured on pages 176–177. Guide discussion of different musical styles, places to listen to music, and the musicians themselves. Explain the NOTES LINGUISTIQUES and NOTES CULTURELLES on TE page 177.

❏   Have students read pages 178–179 as a cooperative group activity. Have groups read and discuss one singing star. As a whole class, invite each group to describe the star and the type of music associated with the star.

❏   Guide students to read the title and subtitles on pages 180–181. Share the information in the NOTES CULTURELLES in the TE margins. Encourage students to discuss musical influences that they recognize and talk about what type of music they enjoy most. As students read pages 180–181, have them suggest which musical influences are common in both American and French music. Use the TEACHING STRATEGY, TE page 181, to encourage students to discuss similarities and differences between music that French young people enjoy and the music that students listen to at home.

### Guided Practice and Checking Understanding

❏   You may check understanding of these readings by asking students to do a short oral summary of each section. Help other students add details to the summaries.

**DAY 2**

## Motivation and Focus

❏ Begin a project based on the *Interlude culturel:* an interdisciplinary music history project or research on one of the artists presented in the text.

## Presentation and Explanation

❏ Have students work in groups to read about francophone music in the Americas, page 182. Explain the NOTES CULTURELLES and NOTES LINGUISTIQUES in the TE margin. Ask groups to explain the different regional music styles and instruments associated with the styles.

❏ Read and discuss the song *Mon pays* on page 183. If possible, play a recording of the song as suggested in the TEACHING STRATEGY, TE page 183. Guide students to point out lines of the song that tie in with the drawing on page 183. Students can share lines from songs that they enjoy that express similar feelings and themes.

❏ Read and discuss the selections on classical music, pages 184–185, encouraging students to talk about pieces and productions they know by these composers. Share the information about the composers in the NOTES CULTURELLES at the bottom of TE pages 184–185.

## Independent Practice

❏ Students can reread the selections independently. Ask them to choose their favorite musical style or musician from the readings and write a paragraph explaining why it is their favorite.

## Monitoring and Adjusting

❏ Monitor students' understanding of the materials in the *Interlude* as they participate in discussions. Have students reread a section that is difficult using a worksheet such as the one shown on TE page T45. Go over the answers in small groups as needed.

## Reteaching (as required)

❏ Have students review any sections that they found difficult. Build background knowledge and give vocabulary explanations to help students as they reread portions of the *Interlude*.

## Extension and Enrichment (as desired)

❏ Students may wish to research Hector Berlioz, Charles Gounod, or other French musicians mentioned in the NOTES CULTURELLES, TE page 185.

❏ For expansion activities, direct students to www.mcdougallittell.com.

## Summary and Closure

❏ Have students present to the class the results of their interdisciplinary music history projects, or their research about one of the musicians. As students share their information, help the class summarize what has been learned about French music.

## Assessment (optional)

❏ Use **Reading and Culture Tests and Quizzes** for *Interlude culturel 4* to assess students' understanding of the information in this section.

# UNITÉ 5: *Bon voyage!, Partie 1,* PAGE 186

## BLOCK SCHEDULE (3 DAYS TO COMPLETE)

### Objectives

| | |
|---|---|
| **Communication Functions and Contexts** | To be able to make travel plans |
| | To be able to go through passport control and customs |
| **Linguistic Goals** | To make negative statements using affirmative and negative expressions |
| **Reading and Cultural Objectives** | To learn what French young people do when they travel and where they go |
| | To read for pleasure |

### Block Schedule

**Personalizing** Students choose two countries they would like to visit. They write the name of their first choice at the top of one half of a piece of paper, and their second choice at the top of the other half. They then write six sentences (using the future) under the first country, explaining what they will do, visit, etc. on their trip. After, they should write the same sentences in the conditional under the second country, changing the information to fit that country.

## DAY 1

### Motivation and Focus

❑ *Unit Opener:* Ask students to look at the photos and illustrations on pages 186–189 and guess where the young people might be going. Read *Thème et Objectifs*, page 186, and discuss favorite vacation destinations for American and French teenagers and how to plan for trips.

❑ *Info Magazine:* Students can browse through pages 187–189 and write down three interesting points to be shared with the class. Discuss the articles, explaining the NOTES CULTURELLES, REALIA NOTES, and NOTES LINGUISTIQUES in the TE margins. Follow the TEACHING STRATEGY suggestions on TE page 188 to help students compare travel activities and destinations of French and American teenagers. Use any or all of the SUJETS DE DISCUSSION on TE page 189. Use the TEACHING STRATEGY on the same page to have students prepare interviews based on the article on page 189. Do *Et vous?*, pages 188 and 189.

### Presentation and Explanation

❑ *Le français pratique (Les voyages):* Model the expressions and vocabulary on pages 190–191 for students to repeat. Guide students to talk about countries they would like to visit and locate the countries on the maps on **Overhead Visuals** Transparencies 2, 3, and 4. Have students read the *Note culturelle,* page 191. Share ADDITIONAL INFORMATION and the NOTE CULTURELLE about French passports and the European Union on TE page 191.

❑ *Langue et communication (Les expressions négatives):* Present the negative expressions with present tense and the *passé composé,* page 192. Model the examples for students to repeat. Guide students to discover the placement of *ne* and the other part of the expressions in relation to the verbs. Optionally, explain the constructions in *Allons plus loin.*

❑ *Langue et communication (L'expression **ne...que**):* Introduce the expression *ne...que* and explain its meaning. Model the examples on page 192 and have students repeat. Explain word order and use of articles after the verb. You may want to use the TEACHING STRATEGY: CHALLENGE on TE page 192 to present the construction *ne faire que.*

### Guided Practice and Checking Understanding

❑ Use the TEACHING STRATEGY, TE page 190, and the maps on **Overhead Visuals** Transparencies 2, 3, and 4 to have students practice talking about countries they'd like to visit and share foreign travel experiences.

❑ Do the TEACHING STRATEGY: WARM-UP on TE page 192 to practice using negative expressions.

❑ Have students do **Practice Activities** pages 133–135 as you play the **Audio,** Cassette 5, Side 1, or read pages 27–29 of the **Cassette Script.**

## DAY 2

### Motivation and Focus

❏ Students can begin planning class trips with the INTERDISCIPLINARY/COMMUNITY CONNECTIONS project described on TE page 207.

### Guided Practice and Checking Understanding

❏ Review **Video** Module 5 Mise en scène. Show the Gros plan, or read from the **Video Script**, and have students do the corresponding activities in the **Video Activity Book**.

### Independent Practice

❏ *Pair activities:* Model the activities on pages 190–193. Students can do activities 1–2 (pages 190–191) and 2–3 (page 193) in pairs. Have students check their work using the **Answer Key**.
❏ *Homework:* Assign activity 1 on page 193.

### Monitoring and Adjusting

❏ Have students complete the writing activities on pages 55–56 of **Practice Activities**.
❏ Monitor use of vocabulary and negative expressions as students work on the practice activities. Refer back to pages 190–192 as needed. Use the NOTES LINGUISTIQUES and TEACHING NOTE, TE page 192, to meet students' needs.

### Reteaching (as needed)

❏ Help students practice identifying and talking about countries with *Appendix A* pages R14–R15.
❏ Use the TEACHING STRATEGY: MULTIPLE INTELLIGENCES, TE page 191, to reteach names, locations, and points of interest in French-speaking countries.

## DAY 3

### Extension and Enrichment (as desired)

❏ For expansion activities, direct students to www.mcdougallittell.com.
❏ Share the information about Swiss cantons in the REALIA NOTES on TE page 190. Students can research the names of the other Swiss cantons or make a map of the cantons.
❏ After explaining the NOTE CULTURELLE about ID forms, TE page 193, have students check newspapers and news reports for information about the EEC.
❏ Have students do the **Block Schedule Activity** at the top of page 39 of these lesson plans.

### Summary and Closure

❏ Show **Overhead Visuals** Transparency 38. Have students choose and describe one of the travelers in the picture and suggest which of the places shown in the brochures the person might visit. Do the Goal 3 activity on page A80. Ask other students to summarize the language and communication goals demonstrated.
❏ Use the STUDENT PORTFOLIOS suggestion on TE page 193 to have students write postcards or letters describing things they did and didn't do, see, like, and eat on a trip to a foreign country.

### Assessment

❏ Use the quiz for *Info Magazine* in **Reading and Culture Tests and Quizzes**. Assess understanding by giving the **Unit Quiz** for *Partie 1*.

# UNITÉ 5: *Bon voyage!, Partie 2,* PAGE 194

## BLOCK SCHEDULE (4 DAYS TO COMPLETE, INCLUDING UNIT TEST)

### Objectives

**Communication Functions and Contexts**
To be able to make travel arrangements and purchase tickets

To be able to travel by plane and by train

**Linguistic Goals**
To use the future tense to talk about future events

To use *si* and *quand* to talk about conditions

To use the conditional to hypothesize about what one would do

**Reading and Cultural Objectives**
To learn why the train is the most popular means of transportation in France

To learn how the Eurotunnel has linked Great Britain and the rest of Europe

To read for information and pleasure

To read illustrated fiction: *Le mystérieux homme en bleu*

> ### Block Schedule
>
> **FunBreak** Have students form groups of 3-4. Each group either brings in a model airplane or draws an illustration of one. Give groups about 10-15 minutes to find the French words for as many parts and areas of the airplane (internal and external) as possible. Groups present the vocabulary they have found and make a list on the board. The group with the longest, most accurate list wins.

---

### DAY 1

### Motivation and Focus

❏ *Info Magazine:* Preview pages 194–195 using the TEACHING STRATEGY, TE page 194. Have students scan the articles, prepare a question about each, and ask their questions for the class to answer. Share the NOTES CULTURELLES (TE pages 194 and 195) and do the INTERDISCIPLINARY CONNECTION (TE page 194). Do the *Et vous?* and *Questions* on pages 194 and 195. Use the TEACHING STRATEGY: CHALLENGE, TE page 195, to compare French and American transportation systems.

### Presentation and Explanation

❏ *Le français pratique (Partons en voyage):* Introduce buying tickets and getting information, pages 196–198. Model the expressions for students to repeat. Use **Overhead Visuals** Transparencies 36, 37, and 38. Read the *Note culturelle,* page 198. Share information in the NOTES CULTURELLES, TE pages 196 and 198.

❏ *Langue et communication (Le futur):* Present the future tense, page 201. Explain how it is formed and have students study the irregular future stems. Use **Overhead Visuals** Transparency 13 to guide students to talk about vacation plans in the future.

### Guided Practice and Checking Understanding

❏ Use **Overhead Visuals** Transparencies 36 and 37 with the Goal 1 activities on pages A75 and A78, or the TEACHING STRATEGY on TE page 196, to practice dialogues about buying tickets and getting travel information.

❏ Check listening skills with the **Audio**, Cassette 5, Side 2, or **Cassette Script** pages 29–32, as students complete activities 1–5 (*le français pratique* – pages 136–137) and *Pratique orale* 1 (*langue et communication* – page 138) of **Practice Activities**.

### Independent Practice

❏ *Pair activities:* Model the activities on pages 199–203. Do 1–6 (pages 199–200) and 1–4 (pages 202–203). Have students check their work in the **Answer Key**.

❏ *Homework:* Assign activity 5 (page 203).

❏ Students can do the additional activities on **Teacher to Teacher** pages 58–64.

DAY 2

## Presentation and Explanation

❑ *Langue et communication (L'usage du futur dans les phrases avec **si**; L'usage du futur après **quand**):* Model and have students repeat the examples of clauses with **si** and **quand** on page 204. Present the use of the future tense in the resultant clause. Introduce conjunctions of time with the *Vocabulaire* box on page 204. Explain the information in the Teaching Strategy: Expansions linguistiques on TE page 204.

❑ *Langue et communication (Le conditionnel):* Do the Warm-Up suggestion on TE page 206. Present the conditional on page 207 using the Teaching Notes in the TE margin. Explain use and formation. Model the examples for students to repeat. Have students create sentences with **si** clauses to complete the Warm-Up activity.

## Guided Practice and Checking Understanding

❑ Check listening skills with the **Audio**, Cassette 5, Side 2, or **Cassette Script** pages 32–33, as students complete *Pratique orale 2–3 (langue et communication* – page 138) of **Practice Activities**.

❑ Review **Video** Module 5. Show *Problème!*, or read it from the **Video Script**, and have students do the *Problème!* and *Supplément* activities in the **Video Activity Book**.

## Independent Practice

❑ *Pair activities:* Model the activities on pages 205–207. Do 7, 9, and 12. Have students check their work in the **Answer Key**.

❑ *Homework:* Assign activities 6 and 8 (page 205), and 10–11 (page 206).

❑ Students can do the additional activities on **Teacher to Teacher** pages 65–68.

## Monitoring and Adjusting

❑ Have students complete the writing activities on pages 58–62 of **Practice Activities**.

❑ As students work on the practice activities, check use of the future, the conditional, and travel vocabulary. Refer to pages 196–207 as needed. Use the appropriate Teaching Strategies on TE pages 199–200 and 204–205.

DAY 3

## Reteaching (as needed)

❑ Review tenses with *Pratique* activities on pages 57 and 60–61 of **Practice Activities**.

## Extension and Enrichment (as desired)

❑ Play the games (TE pages 198 and 201) to practice travel vocabulary and future tense.

❑ Discuss the symbols on page 198 using the Teaching Strategy on TE page 199.

❑ For expansion activities, direct students to www.mcdougallittell.com.

❑ Students can read the mystery story in *Lecture: Le mystérieux homme en bleu*, pages 210–214, or any or all of *Interlude culturel 5*, pages 216–225, for enjoyment or enrichment.

❑ Have students do the **Block Schedule Activity** at the top of page 41 of these lesson plans.

## Summary and Closure

❑ Show **Overhead Visuals** Transparency 38 and use the second Goal 1 activity on page A80 to have students discuss future travel plans. Have other students summarize the communicative and linguistic goals demonstrated.

- ❏ *Lecture (Le mystérieux homme en bleu):* Discuss *Avant de lire*, page 208. Use the TEACHING STRATEGY, TE page 209, to make predictions about the story. Read pages 209–214 in pairs, stopping to answer all *Avez-vous compris?* and *Anticipons un peu!*. Share NOTES CULTURELLES and NOTES LINGUISTIQUES, TE pages 208–214. Help students summarize the story using **Overhead Visuals** Transparency L5. Do the TEACHING STRATEGIES: EXPANSIONS on TE page 215 to review the story. Use the quiz in **Reading and Culture Tests and Quizzes**. Choose any of the oral and written *Après la lecture* activities on page 215.
- ❏ Use any of the STUDENT PORTFOLIOS suggestions on TE pages 203, 206, and 215 for assessment of students' Oral and Written Portfolios.

## Assessment

- ❏ Use the quiz for *Info Magazine* in **Reading and Culture Tests and Quizzes**. Assess understanding of *Partie 2* by administering the corresponding **Unit Quiz**.

### DAY 4

## Reteaching (as needed)

- ❏ Use TEACHING STRATEGIES and ADDITIONAL SITUATIONS for reteaching: TE page 197, transportation vocabulary; TE page 200, asking for information or assistance; TE page 205, talking about circumstances; TE page 206, future; TE page 207, conditional.

## Assessment

- ❏ Use **Unit Test 5** after completing the unit. Choose any of the following **Proficiency Tests**: **Listening Comprehension Performance**, **Speaking Performance**, and **Writing Performance**.

## Notes

## INTERLUDE CULTUREL 5: *Les grands moments de l'histoire de France (1715–1870)*, PAGE 216

### BLOCK SCHEDULE (2 DAYS TO COMPLETE – OPTIONAL)

## Objectives

**Reading Objectives**  To read for content: information about the historical foundation of modern France

To read about the Declaration of the Rights of Man and the French national anthem, *La Marseillaise*

To read a summary of *Les Misérables* by Victor Hugo

**Cultural Objectives**  To learn about the French Revolution and Napoleonic era and important people: Marie-Antoinette, Louis XVI, Napoléon

To learn about French institutions that developed after the revolution: la fête nationale, le drapeau, Marianne, le musée du Louvre, les départements français, le système monétaire, le système métrique, l'armée nationale, l'hymne national

To learn about the French romantic writer and politician Victor Hugo

**Note:** The *Interlude culturel* contains historical background information about the French Revolution and cultural information about French institutions that developed afterwards. The material can be taught as a lesson or introduced in smaller sections as parts of other lessons. The selections can be used to expand cultural awareness, to develop reading skills, to build cultural knowledge, or as resource material for student research projects.

### DAY 1

## Motivation and Focus

❏ As students preview the pictures, maps, titles, and subtitles on pages 216–225, invite them to share information they may know about the people, places, and events pictured. If possible, use the MULTIPLE INTELLIGENCES suggestion, TE page 216, to play recordings of *La Marseillaise* and *Les Misérables*. Discuss the historical periods on the time line, page 216. What events and rulers are on the time line? What was happening in America during this same period?

## Presentation and Explanation

❏ Preview orally the information on pages 216–217 using **Overhead Visuals** Transparencies H3, 1, 1(o), 5, and 5(o). Students can read the pages. Use a worksheet such as the one on TE page T45 to guide students' reading of the text. Discuss the answers. Share the NOTES HISTORIQUES and PHOTO NOTE on TE pages 216–217. Have students compare the map of Europe on page 217 to Transparencies 5 and 5(o). What differences do they see? What borders are different? Which places were separate countries in the 19th century but are now parts of another country? Which places have become separate countries since the 19th century?

❏ Together, read the introductory material about *L'héritage de la Révolution*, page 218. Divide into small groups, with each group reading one or two of the selections on pages 218–221 that describe the French institutions that developed after the revolution. Later, groups can share information that they learned about the French institutions they read about. Share additional information from the NOTES CULTURELLES, ADDITIONAL INFORMATION, and NOTE HISTORIQUE on TE pages 218–221.

## Guided Practice and Checking Understanding

❏ Check understanding of the readings by asking students to do a short oral summary of each section. Guide other students to add more information to the summaries.

## Motivation and Focus

❏ Begin an INTERDISCIPLINARY/COMMUNITY CONNECTIONS project based on the *Interlude culturel;* use the suggestions in TEACHING STRATEGIES, TE page 216.

## Presentation and Explanation

❏ Have students read pages 222–223 to find out the history of the French national anthem, *La Marseillaise.* Guide students to summarize the information, using the time line on page 216 and the map on page 222. Explain the NOTES LINGUISTIQUES in the margins of TE pages 222–223. Use the TEACHING STRATEGIES to discuss students' opinions on changing national anthems, and to compare and contrast the French and American national anthems. Share the NOTE CULTURELLE, TE page 223.

❏ Use the pictures on pages 224–225 to preview Victor Hugo and *Les Misérables.* If possible, play portions of a recording of the musical. Read and discuss the selection. Share the information in the NOTES CULTURELLES and NOTE HISTORIQUE, TE pages 224–225. You may want to explain the ADDITIONAL INFORMATION on TE page 224.

## Independent Practice

❏ Students can reread the selections independently. Ask them to choose their favorite section of the *Interlude culturel* and write a short paragraph explaining why they like this section.

## Monitoring and Adjusting

❏ Refer back to the time line on page 216 after reading each of the selections and ask students to find the section on the time line for the events and people mentioned. Guide discussion of how the events and people were affected by or affected the historical time periods.

## Reteaching (as required)

❏ Have students review any sections that they found difficult. Provide background knowledge and vocabulary explanations to help them understand the readings.

## Extension and Enrichment (as desired)

❏ Students may wish to do further research on the people, events, and institutions mentioned in the *Interlude.*
❏ For expansion activities, direct students to www.mcdougallittell.com.

## Summary and Closure

❏ Students can present the results of their interdisciplinary projects or other research projects they have done for the *Interlude.* As they share their information, help them summarize what they have learned about French history.

## Assessment (optional)

❏ Use **Reading and Culture Tests and Quizzes** for *Interlude culturel 5* to assess students' understanding of the information in this section.

# UNITÉ 6: *Séjour en France, Partie 1,* PAGE 226

## BLOCK SCHEDULE (3 DAYS TO COMPLETE)

### Objectives

**Communication Functions and Contexts**
To be able to decide where to stay when traveling
To be able to reserve a hotel room

**Linguistic Goals**
To use comparative adjectives and adverbs to compare people, things, places, and situations
To use superlatives to make comparisons

**Reading and Cultural Objectives**
To learn about different places you can stay while visiting France
To learn how to use a French guidebook to find a hotel
To read for information

> **Block Schedule**
>
> **FunBreak** Divide the class into small groups. Put the names of several holidays in a paper bag. Each group picks a holiday and brainstorms descriptions of their holiday. They then can read their descriptions to another group. If the other group guesses the holiday correctly, the group describing the holiday gets a point. The team(s) with the most points get extra credit.

### DAY 1

### Motivation and Focus

❑ *Unit Opener:* Have students look through the photos on pages 226–229. Read *Thème et Objectifs*, page 226, and ask students to predict the unit's theme. Use the WARM-UP suggestion on TE page 226 to have students guess the meanings of some cognates. Compare the types of travel accommodations and travel guides pictured to those available in the local area. How can visitors find information about places to stay? Students can share experiences they have had finding accommodations while traveling.

### Presentation and Explanation

❑ *Le français pratique (À l'hôtel):* Present the vocabulary and expressions on pages 230–231 using **Overhead Visuals** Transparency 40. Model the expressions for students to repeat. Do the TEACHING STRATEGY, TE page 230, to have students use the expressions.

### Guided Practice and Checking Understanding

❑ Have students do activities 1–5 (*le français pratique* – pages 139–141) of **Practice Activities** as you play the **Audio**, Cassette 6, Side 1, or read from the **Cassette Script**, pages 33–35.

### Independent Practice

❑ *Pair activities:* Model the activities on pages 232–233. Arrange students in pairs to practice activities 1 and 2 and *Conversations libres.* Have students check their work using the **Answer Key**.

❑ *Homework:* Assign activity 4 (page 233).

### DAY 2

### Motivation and Focus

❑ *Info Magazine:* Have students read page 227. Encourage them to read for information, using cognates and guessing meanings from context. Discuss the range of lodging possibilities and have students talk about their preferences. Share the NOTES CULTURELLES, TE page 227. Bring in a copy of *Le Guide Michelin*. Use **Overhead Visuals** Transparency 39 to preview *Le Guide Michelin*, pages 228–229. Have students read pages 228–229. Explain the NOTES CULTURELLES and NOTE LINGUISTIQUE in the TE margins.

❑ Do *Et vous?* on pages 227 and 229. If students are interested, have them do En voyage: Pour en savoir plus on TE page 229.

❑ Begin planning a local restaurant guide as described in Interdisciplinary/Community Connections on TE page 245. Students can work in small groups on various aspects of the project.

## Presentation and Explanation

❑ *Langue et communication (Le comparatif):* Introduce comparative constructions on page 234. Model the examples and have students repeat. Explain the use of stress pronouns after **que** and the irregular comparative forms. Present the Notes linguistiques on TE page 234.

❑ *Langue et communication (Le superlatif):* Present superlative constructions on page 236. Model the examples and have students repeat. Discuss adjective position and irregular superlative forms. Share the Note linguistique information on TE page 236.

## Guided Practice and Checking Understanding

❑ Use **Overhead Visuals** Transparency 40 and the Review and Practice and Goal 1 activities on pages A84–A85 to practice making reservations, asking for services, and making comparisons.

❑ To check listening, use the **Audio**, Cassette 6, Side 1, or read from **Cassette Script** page 35 as students do the *Pratique orale* 1–2 *(langue et communication* – page 141) of **Practice Activities**.

❑ Show Module 6 of the **Video**, or read from the **Video Script**, and have students do all of the corresponding activities in the **Video Activity Book**. Use the Module 6 suggestion on TE page 235.

## Independent Practice

❑ *Pair activities:* Model the activities on pages 234–237. Arrange students in pairs to practice activities 3, 5, and 7 (pages 235–237). Have students check their work using the **Answer Key**.

❑ *Group activity:* Have students do activity 2 (page 235), and 6 and 8 (page 237) in small groups.

❑ *Homework:* Assign activities 1 (page 234), 4 (page 235), and 9 (page 237).

## Monitoring and Adjusting

❑ Have students complete the writing activities on pages 63–65 of **Practice Activities**.

❑ Monitor use of comparative and superlative constructions and vocabulary about hotel accommodations and information as students work on the practice activities. Refer to pages 230–236 as needed. Do the Teaching Strategies on TE pages 231, 232, 234, 235, and 237, and Expansion on TE page 237, to meet all students' needs.

## DAY 3

## Reteaching (as required)

❑ Redo any of the activities in **Practice Activities** that students found difficult.

## Extension and Enrichment (as desired)

❑ Use the information and vocabulary in Supplementary vocabulary, Realia Notes, Notes linguistiques, Notes culturelles, and Expansion linguistique on TE pages 230–237 to extend the lesson's activities.

❑ Introduce the Proverbes, TE page 234. Students can try writing proverbs they know.

❑ For expansion activities, direct students to www.mcdougallittell.com.

❑ Have students do the **Block Schedule Activity** at the top of page 46 of these lesson plans.

## Summary and Closure

❏ Show **Overhead Visuals** Transparency 40. Ask students to explain which of the hotels they would like to stay at during a vacation. Have others in the class summarize the communicative and linguistic goals demonstrated.

❏ You may want to use the STUDENT PORTFOLIOS suggestion on TE page 233 to have students prepare a brochure to include in their Written Portfolios.

## Assessment

❏ Use the quiz for *Info Magazine* in **Reading and Culture Tests and Quizzes**. Administer the **Unit Quiz** for *Partie 1*.

## Notes

# UNITÉ 6: *Séjour en France, Partie 2,* PAGE 238

## BLOCK SCHEDULE (4 DAYS TO COMPLETE, INCLUDING UNIT TEST)

### Objectives

**Communication Functions and Contexts** To be able to ask for services in a hotel

**Linguistic Goals** To ask for an alternative using the interrogative pronoun *lequel*

To use demonstrative pronouns to point out people or things

To use possessive pronouns

**Reading and Cultural Objectives** To learn about hotel services

To read for enjoyment

To read fiction: a short story

### Block Schedule

**Change of Pace** Plan ahead: Have students bring in hotel guidebooks (from the United States or from a francophone country). Then have them work in small groups to compare their hotels using various adjectives and adverbs.

### DAY 1

### Motivation and Focus

❏  *Info Magazine:* Preview the article by doing the TEACHING STRATEGY on TE page 238. Have students read pages 238–239 for pleasure. Discuss the situations, inviting students to share similar travel/hotel anecdotes. Students can do the oral or written *Et vous?* activities on page 239. Share the NOTES CULTURELLES and NOTES LINGUISTIQUES on TE pages 238–239.

### Presentation and Explanation

❏  *Le français pratique (Services à l'hôtel):* Show **Overhead Visuals** Transparency 41. Model and have students repeat the expressions for asking for services on page 240. Use the TEACHING STRATEGY, TE page 240, to help students create questions for various hotel employees. Do the NOTES LINGUISTIQUES on TE page 240.

❏  *Langue et communication (Le pronom interrogatif lequel; Le pronom démonstratif celui):* Present the interrogative pronoun **lequel** and demonstrative pronoun **celui**, pages 242–243. Model the examples for students to repeat. Explain the meanings of each. Use the TEACHING STRATEGY at the bottom of TE pages 242–243 to guide students to use the pronouns to point out objects in the room.

### Guided Practice and Checking Understanding

❏  Use **Overhead Visuals** Transparencies 41 and 42 with the activities on pages A87–A89 to practice talking about hotel services and asking for assistance.

❏  To check listening comprehension, use the **Audio**, Cassette 6, Side 2, or read the **Cassette Script**, pages 36–38, as students do activities 1–4 (*le français pratique* – pages 142–144) and *Pratique orale* 1–2 (*langue et communication* – page 144) of **Practice Activities**.

❏  Show Module 7 of the **Video**, or read from the **Video Script**, and have students do all of the corresponding activities in the **Video Activity Book**.

### Independent Practice

❏  *Pair activities:* Model the activities on pages 241–243. Arrange students in pairs to do activities 1 (page 241) and 1 and 3 (page 243). Have students check their work using the **Answer Key**. You may want to use the suggestion in TEACHING STRATEGY: EXPANSION (TE page 243).

❏ *Homework:* Assign activity 2 on page 243.

### DAY 2

## Presentation and Explanation

❏ *Langue et communication (Le pronom possessif* **le mien***):* Introduce possessive pronouns, page 244. Model the examples for students to repeat, and explain the use of possessive pronouns in French. You may want to do the Expansion linguistique at the bottom of TE pages 244–245, if appropriate.

## Guided Practice and Checking Understanding

❏ Show Module 7 of the **Video**, or read from the **Video Script**, and have students do all of the corresponding activities in the **Video Activity Book**.
❏ To check listening, use the **Audio**, Cassette 6, Side 2, or read from **Cassette Script** page 38 as students do *Pratique orale* 3 *(langue et communication* – page 144) of **Practice Activities**.

## Independent Practice

❏ *Pair activities:* Model the activities on pages 244–245. Arrange students in pairs to practice activities 4–7. Have students check their work using the **Answer Key**.
❏ Choose any or all of the activities in **Teacher to Teacher**, pages 69–79.

## Monitoring and Adjusting

❏ Have students do the writing activities on pages 66 and 68 of **Practice Activities**.
❏ As students work on the practice activities, monitor use of interrogative, demonstrative, and possessive pronouns and expressions for asking about services. Refer back to the boxes, pages 240–244, as needed. Use the Notes linguistiques in the TE margins.

### DAY 3

## Reteaching (as required)

❏ Reteach possessive pronouns with the *Pratique* activity on **Practice Activities** page 67.
❏ Do the suggestions in Teaching Strategy: Multiple Intelligences, TE page 241, to reteach hotel service vocabulary.

## Extension and Enrichment (as desired)

❏ If students are interested, have them read the story in *Lecture: Une étrange aventure*, pages 247–250, or any of the *Interlude culturel 6* selections, pages 252–259.
❏ Play the game described on page A87 of **Overhead Visuals** with Transparency 41.
❏ For expansion activities, direct students to www.mcdougallittell.com.
❏ Have students do the **Block Schedule Activity** at the top of page 49 of these lesson plans.

## Summary and Closure

❏ Ask pairs of students to role play conversations between hotel guests and the manager in **Overhead Visuals** Transparency 41. Guide other students to summarize the communicative and linguistic goals demonstrated.
❏ *Lecture (Une étrange aventure):* Read and discuss the *Note culturelle* about French villages on page 246. Follow the sugges-

tions in TEACHING STRATEGY, TE page 246, to provide background information about the setting of the story. Use *Avant de lire* to preview the story and help students make predictions. Students can read the story on pages 247–250 independently or in pairs. Encourage students to stop after each section and answer the questions in *Avez-vous compris?* or to make predictions with *Anticipons un peu!*. Use the explanations in NOTES CULTURELLES and NOTES LINGUISTIQUES in the TE margins as needed. Follow the TEACHING STRATEGIES suggestions on TE pages 250 and 251 to guide discussion of the story's ending and to summarize the story. Show **Overhead Visuals** Transparency L6 as a visual aid. You may want to use the quiz for *Lecture* in **Reading and Culture Tests and Quizzes**. Students can work in pairs on any of the oral expression activities in *Après la lecture*, page 251, and do *Expression écrite*, writing a report about France from 1940–1944 or creating a strange story.

❏ Choose any of the suggestions for STUDENT PORTFOLIOS on TE pages 238 (written) or 251 (oral and written). See the suggestions in **Portfolio Assessment**.

## Assessment

❏ Administer the quiz for *Info Magazine* in **Reading and Culture Tests and Quizzes**. Assess understanding of *Partie 2* by using the corresponding **Unit Quiz**.

### DAY 4

## Reteaching (as required)

❏ Redo any of the activities in **Practice Activities** that caused students difficulty.

## Assessment

❏ Have students do **Unit Test 6** after they have completed all of the unit's activities. You may also wish to give any or all of the following **Proficiency Tests** for the unit: **Listening Comprehension Performance**, **Speaking Performance**, and **Writing Performance**.

## Notes

# INTERLUDE CULTUREL 6: *Les grands moments de l'histoire de France (1870–présent)*, PAGE 252

## BLOCK SCHEDULE (2 DAYS TO COMPLETE – OPTIONAL)

### Objectives

**Reading Objectives**    To read for content: information about France in the 20th century

To read a poem: *Liberté* by Paul Éluard

To read a summary of a film: *Au Revoir, les Enfants*

**Cultural Objectives**    To learn about important periods and events of French history

To learn about important people in science and politics: Marie Curie, Jean Moulin, Simone Veil, Charles de Gaulle

To learn about literature and film from 1870 to the present: Paul Éluard, Louis Malle

**Note:** The *Interlude culturel* contains information about French history that can be taught as a lesson or introduced in smaller sections as parts of other lessons. The material in this section can be used to expand cultural awareness, as source material for students' research projects, to develop reading skills, or to build cultural knowledge.

### DAY 1

### Motivation and Focus

❑   Have students look through pages 252–259 and comment on the pictures. Invite students to share information they may know about the people and events pictured. Read the titles and subtitles on each page. Discuss the historical periods on the time line on page 252. What periods are shown? Who are some important people during these times?

### Presentation and Explanation

❑   Show **Overhead Visuals** Transparency H4 as you present an oral preview of the information on page 252. Use the PRE-READING QUESTIONS on TE page 252 to focus students as they read page 252. Guide discussion of the reading. What artistic movements began in France during **La Belle Époque**? How was France involved in the two World Wars? What French colonies became independent in the modern period? How has Europe become more united? Share the information in the NOTES HISTORIQUES and NOTES CULTURELLES and use POUR EN SAVOIR PLUS to encourage students to look at other *Interludes* for additional information, TE page 252.

❑   Students can work in small groups to read about the people on page 253. Have groups read about different people. Then invite each group to present information about their person. As you summarize the readings, share additional information from NOTES CULTURELLES on TE page 252.

❑   Ask students to describe Charles de Gaulle in the photos and illustrations on pages 254–255. Guide students to notice the air of authority and leadership qualities of de Gaulle. After students read the pages, including *Documents*, have them compare de Gaulle's life and influence on France to that of an American leader. Share the NOTES CULTURELLES, ADDITIONAL INFORMATION, and REALIA NOTES in the TE margins.

### Guided Practice and Checking Understanding

❑   Check understanding of the readings by asking students to prepare short oral summaries for each of the sections. Help others add information to the summaries.

DAY 2

## Motivation and Focus

❏ Help students plan a project based on *Interlude culturel 6*. Students can choose one of the people or events presented to create an interdisciplinary project including science, history, literature, art, and/or film.

## Presentation and Explanation

❏ Together, read the introduction to *Liberté, liberté* and the information about Paul Éluard on page 256. Encourage students to talk about what liberty or freedom means to them. Read aloud the poem on page 257 as students follow along in their books. Use the TEACHING STRATEGIES, TE page 257, to guide discussion of the poem. Students might want to suggest other places where they would write the word ***liberté***. If students are interested, read the middle part of the poem À NOTER, TE page 257. Students can review information about surrealism, following the suggestions in POUR EN SAVOIR PLUS on TE page 256.

❏ Have students read the introduction to *Au Revoir, les Enfants* on pages 256–257. You may want to share the information in the LANGUAGE NOTES and ANECDOTE in the TE margin of page 256. Read and discuss the summary of the film. Encourage students to use the photos to help understand the action. You may want to show portions of the film. See the information about using feature-length films on TE pages T50–T51, and the IMPORTANT TEACHING NOTE on TE page 258 about previewing and carefully considering portions to show. Share the ADDITIONAL INFORMATION, NOTE CULTURELLE, and NOTE LINGUISTIQUE on TE pages 258–259.

## Independent Practice

❏ Students can reread the selections independently. Ask them to choose their favorite selection or person presented in the readings and write a short paragraph explaining their choice.

## Monitoring and Adjusting

❏ Ask each student to prepare a question to share with the class about any of the *Interlude culturel 6* selections. Monitor understanding as students discuss the answers to the questions.

## Reteaching (as required)

❏ Have students review any sections that they found difficult. Provide background knowledge and vocabulary explanations to help them understand the readings.

## Extension and Enrichment (as desired)

❏ Use the TEACHING STRATEGY, TE page 256, to provide additional readings and music of the ***Résistance***.
❏ If students are interested, have them interview family members or friends about World War II experiences and remembrances as suggested in the TEACHING STRATEGY, TE page 254.
❏ For expansion activities, direct students to www.mcdougallittell.com.

## Summary and Closure

❏ Encourage students to share the results of their interdisciplinary projects. As students present their findings to the class, help summarize what they have learned about the period of French history from 1870 to the present.

## Assessment (optional)

❏ Use **Reading and Culture Tests and Quizzes** for *Interlude culturel 6* to assess students' understanding of the information in this section.

# UNITÉ 7: *La forme et la santé, Partie 1,* PAGE 260

## BLOCK SCHEDULE (3 DAYS TO COMPLETE)

### Objectives

**Communication Functions and Contexts**
To be able to go to a doctor's office

To be able to describe symptoms and explain what is wrong

To be able to follow the doctor's instructions

**Linguistic Goals**
To use the subjunctive to express how you and others feel about certain facts or events

To use the subjunctive to express fear, doubt, disbelief

**Reading and Cultural Objectives**
To learn how the French take care of their health

To learn why the French drink mineral water

To read for information

> **Block Schedule**
>
> **Variety** Have students work in pairs to write a letter to an advice columnist. They must use at least 4 of the verbs and expressions of emotion on p. 272. Students must also write an answer to the letter. Display the letters on the bulletin board.

### DAY 1

## Motivation and Focus

❏ *Unit Opener:* Ask students to look at the photos on pages 260–262, read *Thème et Objectifs,* and suggest the content of the unit. Students can discuss health issues. Where can people get medical care? How is medical care paid for? What health foods and drinks are available? What herbal medicines do students know? Are they effective?

❏ *Info Magazine:* Use the suggestions in TEACHING STRATEGY, TE page 261, to guide students as they read pages 261–262. Explain the NOTE CULTURELLE and NOTES LINGUISTIQUES in the TE margins. Use the TEACHING STRATEGY, TE page 262, to review the information in the articles. Do the debates in *Et vous?*, page 261. Additional topics can be found in DÉBATS, TE page 261. Use **Overhead Visuals** Transparencies 1 and 1(o) to help students locate the French spas mentioned on page 262. Share ADDITIONAL INFORMATION, TE page 262. Students can do the *Et vous?* project about mineral waters, page 262. Have students work in pairs or small groups to discuss and answer the questions in *Le savez-vous?*, page 263. You may want to share the information in the NOTES LINGUISTIQUES and NOTES CULTURELLES on TE page 263.

## Presentation and Explanation

❏ *Le français pratique (Une visite médicale):* Model and have students repeat the expressions on pages 264–266. Use **Overhead Visuals** Transparency 43 with the TEACHING STRATEGY, TE page 265, to talk about health and remedies.

❏ *Langue et communication (Le concept du subjonctif: temps et modes):* Introduce mood and tense of verbs, page 270. Explain the use of the subjunctive mood to express feelings and emotions, using the cartoon at the bottom of page 270. Model the examples for students to repeat. Use the suggestion at the bottom of TE page 270 to use **Video** Module 8 to familiarize students with the subjunctive.

❏ *Langue et communication (Les verbes **croire** et **craindre**):* Present irregular forms of the verbs, page 271. Use the TEACHING STRATEGY, TE page 271, to talk about fears.

## Guided Practice and Checking Understanding

❏ Use **Overhead Visuals** Transparencies 43 and 44 with the activities on page A91–A95 to practice doctor–patient conversations and to talk about emotions and feelings.

❏ Have students do activities 1–4 (*le français pratique* – pages 145–146) and *Pratique orale* 1–3 (*langue et communication* – pages 146–147) of **Practice Activities** as you play the **Audio**, Cassette 7, Side 1, or read from the **Cassette Script**, pages 39–41.

## Independent Practice

❏ *Pair activities:* Model the activities on pages 267–271. Arrange students in pairs to do activities 1 and 3 and *Conversations libres* (pages 267–269), and activity 1 (page 271). Have students check their work using the **Answer Key**.

❏ *Homework:* Assign activity 4 (page 268).

### DAY 2

## Motivation and Focus

❏ Help students begin planning the INTERDISCIPLINARY/COMMUNITY CONNECTIONS project on TE page 281. Students can work in groups on various aspects of the project.

## Presentation and Explanation

❏ *Langue et communication (L'usage du subjonctif: émotions et sentiments):* Explain use of the subjunctive to express emotions and feelings, page 272. Model the expressions in the *Vocabulaire* box on page 272 for students to repeat. Use the TEACHING STRATEGY in the side margin of TE page 272 to help students create sentences about the pictures in the box.

❏ *Langue et communication (Le subjonctif après les expressions de doute):* Present the expressions of certainty and doubt in the *Vocabulaire* box on page 275. Explain use of the indicative with expressions of certainty and the subjunctive with expressions of doubt, page 274.

## Guided Practice and Checking Understanding

❏ Have students do *Pratique orale* 4 *(langue et communication* – page 147) of **Practice Activities** as you play the **Audio**, Cassette 7, Side 1, or read from the **Cassette Script**, page 41.

❏ Show the Mise en scène and Gros plan sections of **Video** Module 8, or read from the **Video Script**. Do the corresponding activities in the **Video Activity Book**.

## Independent Practice

❏ *Pair activities:* Model the activities on pages 272–275. Arrange students in pairs to do activities 3 and 6 (pages 273 and 275). Have students check their work using the **Answer Key**.

❏ *Homework:* Assign activities 4 and 5 (page 273), and 7 (page 275).

❏ Do any of the additional activities in **Teacher to Teacher**, pages 80–82 and 86–89.

## Monitoring and Adjusting

❏ Have students do the writing activities on pages 69–73 of **Practice Activities**.

❏ Monitor use of the subjunctive, expressions of emotion and doubt, and health-related vocabulary as students work on the practice activities. Refer to the boxes on pages 264–266 and 270–275. Do the TEACHING STRATEGIES on TE pages 265–274.

### DAY 3

## Reteaching (as required)

❏ Use the *Reference* section of the textbook as needed for reteaching: *Appendix A* page R12 for body parts, and *Appendix C* pages R19, R21, and R23–R31 for forming the subjunctive.

## Extension and Enrichment (as desired)

❏ Share the NOTES CULTURELLES, NOTES LINGUISTIQUES, ADDITIONAL INFORMATION, and ANECDOTE (TE pages 264, 267, 269, and 275) about medical discoveries and information. Students can research any of these topics and share their findings with the class.

❏ For expansion activities, direct students to www.mcdougallittell.com.

❏ Have students do the **Block Schedule Activity** at the top of page 54 of these lesson plans.

## Summary and Closure

❏ Use **Overhead Visuals** Transparency 43. Have students suggest what the problems are and what the doctor might recommend to each of the patients. Guide students to summarize the vocabulary, language, and communication goals demonstrated.

❏ Use students' dialogues in activity 2, page 267, for Oral Portfolios. Follow the suggestions in STUDENT PORTFOLIOS on TE page 267.

## Assessment

❏ Use the quiz for *Info Magazine* in **Reading and Culture Tests and Quizzes**. Assess understanding by administering the **Unit Quiz** for *Partie 1*.

## Notes

# UNITÉ 7: *La forme et la santé, Partie 2,* PAGE 276

## BLOCK SCHEDULE (4 DAYS TO COMPLETE, INCLUDING UNIT TEST)

### Objectives

**Communication Functions and Contexts**
To be able to explain what is wrong to a doctor
To be able to go to the dentist's office
To be able to go to the emergency room

**Linguistic Goals**
To use the past subjunctive to express feelings or attitudes about past actions and events

**Reading and Cultural Objectives**
To learn how the French help provide health care to less fortunate people around the world
To read for enjoyment
To read a short story: *En Voyage* by Guy de Maupassant

> **Block Schedule**
>
> **Change of Pace** Encourage students to research health and fitness opportunities in France and other francophone countries via the Internet or with a local travel agency.

### DAY 1

### Motivation and Focus

❑ *Info Magazine:* Have students preview the article on pages 276–277 by looking at the photos and reading the titles and captions. Follow the TEACHING STRATEGY suggestions on TE page 276 to guide students as they scan and discuss the article. Share the information in the NOTES CULTURELLES, TE pages 276–277. Have students work in pairs on the definitions in *Et vous?*, page 277. Students can write letters for the *Expression écrite* part of *Et vous?*. You may want to do the EXPANSION suggestion on TE page 277.

### Presentation and Explanation

❑ *Le français pratique (Accidents et soins dentaires):* Model and have students repeat the expressions and vocabulary for talking about accidents, emergency care, and the dentist, pages 278–279. Use **Overhead Visuals** Transparencies 45 and 46 to clarify meanings. Use the TEACHING STRATEGY suggestion at the bottom of TE page 278 to have students write group stories.

❑ *Langue et communication (Le passé du subjonctif):* Introduce the past subjunctive on page 280. Model the examples for students to repeat. Explain that it is a compound tense. Guide students to discover the two parts: present subjunctive of **avoir** or **être** and the past participle. Remind students about agreement with past participles with the TEACHING STRATEGY in the side margin of TE page 280.

### Guided Practice and Checking Understanding

❑ Use **Overhead Visuals** Transparencies 45 and 46 and the Review and Practice activities on pages A96 and A99 to practice talking about injuries and other medical problems and giving advice.

❑ Have students do pages 148–150 of **Practice Activities** as you play the **Audio**, Cassette 7, Side 2, or read from the **Cassette Script**, pages 42–44.

### Independent Practice

❑ *Pair activities:* Model the activities on pages 278–281. Arrange students in pairs to practice activities 1–2 and *Conversations libres* (pages 278–279) and 1–2 and 4 (pages 280–281). Students can check their work using the **Answer Key**. Use the TEACHING STRATEGY information, TE page 281, when doing activity 4.

❑ *Homework:* Assign activity 3 on page 281.

### DAY 2

## Guided Practice and Checking Understanding

❑ Review **Video** Module 8. Show the Problème! section, or read from the **Video Script**, and have students do the Problème! and Supplément activities in the **Video Activity Book**.

❑ Practice present and past subjunctive with the TPR activity on TE page 280.

## Independent Practice

❑ Do any of the additional activities in **Teacher to Teacher**, pages 83–85 and 90–93.

## Monitoring and Adjusting

❑ Have students do the writing activities on pages 74–76 of **Practice Activities**.

❑ As students work on the practice activities, monitor use of the past subjunctive and expressions for dental and emergency care. Refer students to pages 278–280 as needed. Use the TEACHING STRATEGY suggestions on TE page 279 to meet all students' needs.

### DAY 3

## Extension and Enrichment (as desired)

❑ For expansion activities, direct students to www.mcdougallittell.com.

❑ Assign the short story in *Lecture: En voyage*, pages 283–290, for reading enjoyment, or allow students to read any of the selections in *Interlude culturel 7*, pages 292–301.

❑ You may want to introduce the SUPPLEMENTARY VOCABULARY in the margins of TE pages 278–279.

❑ Have students do the **Block Schedule Activity** at the top of page 57 of these lesson plans.

## Summary and Closure

❑ Have students do the Goal 1 activities on pages A97 and A99 of **Overhead Visuals**. Use Transparencies 45 and 46 as visual aids. Guide other students to summarize the communicative and linguistic goals demonstrated.

❑ *Lecture (En voyage):* Read about Guy de Maupassant and the information about the story's setting in *Avant de lire*, page 282. Use *Anticipons un peu!*, page 282, to help students make predictions about the story. Have students read the story on pages 283–290, using the TEACHING STRATEGIES at the bottom of TE pages 282–290 and Transparency L7 to guide discussion and clarify the events of the story. Students can answer the *Avez-vous compris?* and *Anticipons un peu!* questions throughout. Explain the information in the NOTES CULTURELLES and NOTES LINGUISTIQUES in the TE margins. Use the quiz for *Lecture* in **Reading and Culture Tests and Quizzes**. As a closing activity, have students do any of the *Après la lecture* oral and written activities on page 291.

❑ Students can prepare either the *Situations* or *Expression écrite* activities for inclusion in their portfolios. Follow the suggestions in STUDENT PORTFOLIOS on TE page 291.

## Assessment

❑ Use the quiz for *Info Magazine* in **Reading and Culture Tests and Quizzes**. Assess understanding by administering the **Unit Quiz** for *Partie 2*.

DAY 4

## Reteaching (as required)

❏ Reteach sections that students found difficult. Then have students redo any activities for reinforcement.

## Assessment

❏ Administer **Unit Test 7** after completing all of the unit's activities. You may also wish to give any or all of the **Proficiency Tests** for the unit: **Listening Comprehension Performance**, **Speaking Performance**, and **Writing Performance**.

## Notes

# INTERLUDE CULTUREL 7: *Les français d'aujourd'hui*, PAGE 292

## BLOCK SCHEDULE (2 DAYS TO COMPLETE – OPTIONAL)

### Objectives

**Reading Objectives**    To read for content: information about modern France as a multi-ethnic and multi-cultural society

To read a song: *Éthiopie*

**Cultural Objectives**    To learn about the French as citizens of Europe

To learn about French humanitarians: L'abbé Pierre, Coluche

To learn about the new French mosaic: the impact of immigration on French society

To learn about the ***Maghrébins***: their culture and their religion

To learn about **SOS Racisme**

**Note:** The *Interlude culturel* contains cultural information about contemporary French society. It can be taught as a lesson or introduced in smaller sections as parts of other lessons. The material in this section can be used to expand cultural awareness, as source material for students' research projects, to develop reading skills, or to build cultural knowledge.

### DAY 1

### Motivation and Focus

❏   Ask students to look through the maps and photos on pages 292–301. Students can comment on the various types of people represented in the photos. Read the titles and subtitles on each page. Discuss the racial and ethnic make-up of French society and France's role in Europe. What countries have recent immigrants come from? What is the European Union? What advantages might a united Europe provide for Europeans?

### Presentation and Explanation

❏   Preview the information on page 292, using **Overhead Visuals** Transparencies 5 and 5(o) to present member countries of the European Union. After students read page 292 and *Les symboles de l'Europe* on page 293, guide discussion of the reading. What is the European Union? How has the European community helped France? What were some of the important stages in the unification process? Share the information in the NOTES CULTURELLES on TE page 292 and the REALIA NOTE on TE page 293.

❏   You may want to divide the class into groups to read the four views on the European Union on page 293. Each group can explain the views of the person they read about. Explain the information about Erasme in the NOTE CULTURELLE, TE page 293. As a class, summarize the advantages mentioned. Encourage students to comment on which advantages they think are most important.

❏   Ask students to guess the type of work started by the two humanitarians shown on pages 294–295. Have students read to find out how and why L'abbé Pierre and Coluche began their social work. Share the NOTES CULTURELLES in the TE margins. Students may want to look back at pages 252–259 to review information about the ***Résistance***. Compare the organizations and types of services provided by ***Chiffonniers d'Emmaüs*** and ***Restaurants du coeur*** to local community organizations that provide services.

❏   Have students read pages 296–300 to find out about the impact of immigration on French society and about the culture and religion of the ***Maghrébins***. Use **Overhead Visuals** Transparency 4 to help students locate the countries of origin of recent immigrant groups to France. Share the information in NOTES CULTURELLES, NOTES HISTORIQUES, REALIA NOTE, NOTES LINGUISTIQUES, and ADDITIONAL INFORMATION in the TE margins. Guide students to summarize the information. If appropriate, students can compare the immigrant groups and their influence in the U.S. to those in France. You may want to use the TEACHING STRATEGY on TE page 300 to have students role play an interview between a journalist and **SOS Racisme** founder Harlem Désir.

## Guided Practice and Checking Understanding

❑ Check understanding of the readings by asking students to do a short oral summary of each section. Help other students add information to the summaries.

## Independent Practice

❑ Students can reread the selections independently. Ask them to choose a person or social issue from the readings and write a short paragraph explaining the person's or issue's importance.

### DAY 2

## Motivation and Focus

❑ Begin a project based on *Interlude culturel 7*. Students may want to research the European Union, one of the humanitarians presented in the *Interlude*, or immigration.

## Presentation and Explanation

❑ Present the song on page 301, using the NOTE CULTURELLE in the TE margin to provide background information on Ethiopia. Encourage students to share information they know about the plight of Ethiopian children due to famine and civil war. Read the song as students follow along in their books. Guide discussion of the images evoked in the song. If the class is interested, try singing the song using the tune of *We Are the World*. Use the TEACHING STRATEGY, TE page 301, to have students prepare logos and mottoes about peace and tolerance.

## Monitoring and Adjusting

❑ Monitor students' understanding of the selections as they discuss the content and prepare summaries. Help students go back through the readings to find information.

## Reteaching (as required)

❑ Have students review any sections that they found difficult. Provide background information and vocabulary explanations to help them understand the readings.

## Extension and Enrichment (as desired)

❑ If students are interested, have them prepare a project on immigration as described in the TEACHING STRATEGY on TE page 296.
❑ For expansion activities, direct students to www.mcdougallittell.com.

## Summary and Closure

❑ Have students share with the class the results of their research projects about the European Union and francophone African countries. As students make their presentations, help them summarize what they have learned about the multi-ethnic diversity of French society and the role of France as part of Europe.

## Assessment (optional)

❑ Use **Reading and Culture Tests and Quizzes** for *Interlude 7* to assess students' understanding of the reading selections.

# UNITÉ 8: *En ville, Partie 1,* PAGE 302

## BLOCK SCHEDULE (2 DAYS TO COMPLETE)

### Objectives

| | |
|---|---|
| **Communication Functions and Contexts** | To make a date or arrange to meet friends at a specific time and place |
| **Linguistic Goals** | To use the imperfect to make wishes or suggestions |
| | To use the imperfect and pluperfect to narrate past actions in sequence |
| **Reading and Cultural Objectives** | To learn how French cities developed historically |
| | To learn about the advantages and disadvantages of urban life |
| | To read for information |

> **Block Schedule**
>
> **Retention** Have students write a journal entry on what they would do with a million dollars. **Que ferais-tu si tu étais multi-millionaire?** They can discuss how they would change the world or what they would do to impove the environment.

### DAY 1

### Motivation and Focus

❏ *Unit Opener:* Have students look at the photos on pages 302–305 and describe the cities and aspects of city life pictured. Read *Thème et Objectifs,* page 302, and help students make predictions about the theme of the unit. Encourage students to give their opinions of city life. What can you do in the city? What are the good and bad points about living in cities? What difference might you expect to see between French and American cities?

❏ *Info Magazine:* Have students read page 303 using the TEACHING STRATEGY suggestions, TE page 303. Share the ADDITIONAL INFORMATION in the TE margin about the history of French cities. Use **Overhead Visuals** Transparencies 1 and 1(o) to review names and locations of French cities. Review American cities with French origins by having students do the INTERDISCIPLINARY/ COMMUNITY CONNECTIONS activity on TE page 310. Share the NOTES CULTURELLES, TE page 304. Read and discuss the articles on pages 304–305. Students can do the self-quiz activity and share their scores in small groups. Do the TEACHING STRATEGIES, TE pages 304–305, and *Et vous?*, page 303.

❏ Help students begin work on the INTERDISCIPLINARY/COMMUNITY CONNECTIONS project on TE page 325. Students can work in small groups to prepare a tourist poster illustrating activities available in the local area.

### Presentation and Explanation

❏ *Le français pratique (Un rendez-vous en ville):* Model and have students repeat the expressions in the boxes on pages 306–307. Do the TEACHING STRATEGY at the bottom of TE page 306 to help students use the expressions to write a group story.

❏ *Langue et communication (La construction si + imparfait):* Present the use of *si + imparfait* to express wishes or suggestions, page 308. Model the examples for students to repeat. Use the TEACHING STRATEGY: WARM-UP, TE page 308, to have students express wishes using the imperfect. Explain the NOTES LINGUISTIQUES.

❏ *Langue et communication (Le plus-que-parfait):* Introduce the pluperfect, page 308. Explain its use to describe what someone had done or what had happened before another action. Model the forms, guiding students to notice the agreement of the past participle. Do the TEACHING STRATEGY, TE page 309, to have students work in groups using the pluperfect to describe past actions.

### Guided Practice and Checking Understanding

❏ Use **Overhead Visuals** Transparency 47 and the activities on p. A101 to help students practice making plans to get together.

❏ Have students do pages 151–152 of **Practice Activities** as you play the **Audio**, Cassette 8, Side 1, or read from the **Cassette Script**, pages 45–47.

❑ Show the Mise en scène section of **Video** Module 9, or read from the **Video Script**, and have students do the corresponding activities in the **Video Activity Book**.

## Independent Practice

❑ *Pair activities:* Model the activities on pages 306–309. Students can work in pairs on activity 1 and *Conversations libres* (pages 306–307) and activity 1 (page 309). Have students check their work using the **Answer Key**.

❑ *Homework:* Assign activities 2 and 4 on page 309 for homework.

### DAY 2

## Monitoring and Adjusting

❑ Have students do the writing activities on pages 77–79 of **Practice Activities**.

❑ As students work on the practice activities, monitor use of *si* + the imperfect, the pluperfect, and vocabulary and expressions for arranging dates. Refer students back to the boxes on pages 306–308 as needed. Do the TEACHING STRATEGY on TE page 307.

## Reteaching (as required)

❑ Reteach the formation of the imperfect tense using the *Reference* section of the textbook, *Appendix A* page R5.

❑ See *Unité 1*, page 44, to reteach reflexive verbs.

## Extension and Enrichment (as desired)

❑ Use the SUPPLEMENTARY VOCABULARY, TE page 307, to extend the practice activities.

❑ For expansion activities, direct students to www.mcdougallittell.com.

❑ Students can read any of the *Interlude culturel 8* selections, pages 334–343, for information.

❑ Have students do the **Block Schedule Activity** at the top of page 62 of these lesson plans.

## Summary and Closure

❑ Show **Overhead Visuals** Transparency 47 and have students do the Goal 1 activities on page A101. As students present the conversations and explain their preferences, guide others to summarize the communicative and linguistic goals demonstrated.

❑ Record any of the *Conversations libres* on page 307 for inclusion in students' Oral Portfolios. See the suggestions and forms in **Portfolio Assessment**.

## Assessment

❑ Use the quiz for *Info Magazine* in **Reading and Culture Tests and Quizzes**. Use the **Unit Quiz** for *Partie 1* as appropriate.

## UNITÉ 8: *En ville, Partie 2,* PAGE 310

### BLOCK SCHEDULE (2 DAYS TO COMPLETE)

## Objectives

| | |
|---|---|
| **Communication Functions and Contexts** | To explain where one lives and how to get there |
| | To describe one's neighborhood |
| **Linguistic Goals** | To use the conditional to talk about what one would do in certain circumstances |
| | To use the conditional to formulate polite requests |
| **Reading and Cultural Objectives** | To learn what a typical French city looks like |
| | To read for information and enjoyment |

### Block Schedule

**FunBreak** Start the class by having a tape recorder ready and several strips of paper with situations on them. Hand out the situations one by one and give each student 2 minutes to prepare a speech. Example situations could include: *You are traveling to Europe for 2 weeks. What would you take?* Or *You have just found a wallet with a lot of money. What would you do?* Have them speak for 2 minutes.

DAY 1

## Motivation and Focus

❑ *Info Magazine:* Show **Overhead Visuals** Transparencies 6, 48, and 48(o) and read about and discuss the various sections of French cities in *La géographie des villes françaises,* pages 310–311. Encourage students to comment on the types of buildings pictured and guess the types of activities that predominate in each of the city sections. Do the TEACHING STRATEGY on TE page 311 and *Et vous?* on page 311. Share the information in the ANECDOTE, NOTES CULTURELLES, and NOTES LINGUISTIQUES in the TE margins.

❑ Students can continue to work on the INTERDISCIPLINARY/COMMUNITY CONNECTIONS project comparing French and U.S. cities and towns. Suggested procedures are described on TE page 310.

## Presentation and Explanation

❑ *Le français pratique (Comment expliquer où on habite):* Show **Overhead Visuals** Transparencies 48 and 49 as you model the expressions for describing locations and names of city places for students to repeat, pages 312–313. Guide students to talk about where they live. Do the housing interview suggestion in TEACHING STRATEGY, TE page 312.

❑ *Langue et communication (Révision: le conditionnel):* Review formation and use of the conditional to express what would happen, page 314. You may want to use **Video** Module 9, following the suggestions on TE page 314, to help students review uses of the conditional.

❑ *Langue et communication (Le conditionnel dans des phrases avec si):* Explain the use of the conditional with *si* clauses, page 316. Model the examples for students to repeat. Do the TEACHING STRATEGY, TE page 316, to help students use the conditional with *si* and conditions.

❑ *Langue et communication (Le conditionnel: autres usages):* Introduce other uses of the conditional, page 318. Use the TEACHING STRATEGY in the side margin of TE page 318 to explain the use of ***pouvoir*** in the conditional for making polite requests. Explain about indirect speech using the NOTE LINGUISTIQUE, TE page 318. Model the examples and have students repeat.

## Guided Practice and Checking Understanding

❑ Use the TEACHING STRATEGIES at the bottom of TE pages 318–319 to help students practice using the conditional with indirect speech and to write a group story containing examples of the different uses of the conditional.

❑ Have students do pages 153–157 of **Practice Activities** as you play the **Audio**, Cassette 8, Side 2, or read from the **Cassette Script**, pages 47–50.

❑ Review **Video** Module 9. Show the Gros plan section, or read from the **Video Script**, and have students do the corresponding activities in the **Video Activity Book**.

## Independent Practice

❏ *Pair activities:* Model the activities on pages 312–319. Students can do activities 1–2 (pages 312–313) and 1–3, 7, and 9–11 (pages 314–319) in pairs. Have them check their work in the **Answer Key**. You may want to use the TEACHING STRATEGY and EXPANSION suggestions on TE pages 314–317 for activities 1, 2, and 8.

❏ *Homework:* Assign activities 4 (page 315) and 8 (page 317) for homework.

❏ *Group activities:* Students can practice activities 5 and 6 on page 316 in small groups.

❏ Do the **Teacher to Teacher** activity, pages 94–96.

### DAY 2

## Monitoring and Adjusting

❏ Have students do the writing activities on pages 80–83 of **Practice Activities**.

❏ As students work on the practice activities, monitor use of the conditional and city vocabulary. Refer to the boxes on pages 312–318 as needed. Do the TEACHING STRATEGY: MULTIPLE INTELLIGENCES on TE page 315 to meet all students' needs.

## Reteaching (as required)

❏ Use the *Reference* section of the textbook as needed for reteaching: *Appendix A* page R10 for numbers, and *Appendix C* page R19 for formation of the conditional.

## Extension and Enrichment (as desired)

❏ Play the game in TEACHING STRATEGY, TE page 313, to have students write definitions and guess vocabulary words.

❏ Introduce additional cultural material related to housing and city life. Use the NOTES CULTURELLES and TEACHING NOTE, TE page 312, for French street names and HLMs. Read the *Flash d'information* on page 313 and share the NOTE CULTURELLE in the TE margin about the French gendarmes. Use the NOTE CULTURELLE, TE page 316, to describe attractions at *Le Parc de la Villette*. Explain information about the French phone system with the NOTE CULTURELLE, TE page 319.

❏ For expansion activities, direct students to www.mcdougallittell.com.

❏ Have students do the **Block Schedule Activity** at the top of page 64 of these lesson plans.

## Summary and Closure

❏ Show **Overhead Visuals** Transparency 49 and have students do the Goal 1 activity on page A106. As students talk about places on the map, guide others to summarize the communicative and linguistic goals demonstrated.

❏ You may want to use the oral conversations in activity 2, page 313, or the paragraph about vacations in activity 4, page 315, for students' Oral and Written Portfolios. Use the suggestions and forms in **Portfolio Assessment**.

## Assessment

❏ Use the quiz for *Info Magazine* in **Reading and Culture Tests and Quizzes**. Use the **Unit Quiz** for *Partie 2* as appropriate.

# UNITÉ 8: *En ville, Partie 3*, PAGE 320

## BLOCK SCHEDULE (4 DAYS TO COMPLETE, INCLUDING UNIT TEST)

### Objectives

**Communication Functions and Contexts** To discuss city life

**Linguistic Goals** To use the past conditional to hypothesize about what one would do under certain circumstances

**Reading and Cultural Objectives** To learn what types of street artists you might see in Paris or other large cities

To read for enjoyment

To read a short story: *Les pêches* by André Theuriet

#### Block Schedule

**Process Time** Allow students time to look back through the unit and review the vocabulary and grammatical concepts that have been covered. Ask them to share what they found interesting, helpful, easy, difficult, etc. For grammatical concepts, have students who found a particular concept easy explain it to those who found it difficult.

### DAY 1

### Motivation and Focus

❏ *Info Magazine:* Have students preview the articles on pages 320–321. Use the TEACHING STRATEGY suggestions on TE page 320 to guide students' reading for pleasure. Share the NOTE CULTURELLE and ADDITIONAL INFORMATION in the margin of TE page 320. Students can compare the street entertainment mentioned in the articles to that in the local area. Do the TEACHING STRATEGY: EXPANSION, TE page 321, and the *Et vous?* activities on page 321.

### Presentation and Explanation

❏ *Langue et communication (Le conditionnel passé):* Present the use of the past conditional to express what would have happened under certain circumstances, page 322. Explain the information about the uses of the past conditional in the NOTE LINGUISTIQUE, TE page 322. Model the examples for students to repeat. Do the suggestion in TEACHING STRATEGY, TE page 322, to have students use the past conditional. You may want to discuss the past conditional of ***vouloir***, ***pouvoir***, and ***devoir*** in *Allons plus loin,* page 323.

### Guided Practice and Checking Understanding

❏ Use the TEACHING STRATEGY: EXPANSION, TE page 323, to have students discuss and write about what would have happened in various situations. Follow the suggestions in TEACHING STRATEGY: REVIEW, TE page 324, to help students with the different tenses.

### Independent Practice

❏ *Pair activities:* Model the activities on pages 323–324. Students can work in pairs on activities 1–4. Have them check their answers in the **Answer Key**.

❏ Do any of the additional activities in **Teacher to Teacher**, pages 97–104.

### DAY 2

### Presentation and Explanation

❏ *Langue et communication (Résumé: l'usage des temps avec **si**):* Review the sequence of tenses with ***si*** on page 324. Model the examples for students to repeat. Guide students to discover the tenses used in the different clauses. You may want to use the NOTE LINGUISTIQUE, TE page 324, to explain modifications of the sequence of tenses.

## Guided Practice and Checking Understanding

❑ Have students do page 158 of **Practice Activities** as you play the **Audio**, Cassette 8, Side 2, or read from the **Cassette Script**, pages 50–51.

❑ Review **Video** Module 9. Show the Problème! section and have students do the Problème! and Supplément activities in the **Video Activity Book**.

## Independent Practice

❑ *Pair activities:* Model the activities on page 325. Students can work in pairs on activities 5 and 7. Have them check their answers in the **Answer Key**.

❑ *Homework:* Assign activities 6 and 8 (page 325).

❑ Do any of the additional activities in **Teacher to Teacher**, pages 97–104.

### DAY 3

## Monitoring and Adjusting

❑ Have students do the writing activities on pages 84–86 of **Practice Activities**.

❑ Check use of the past conditional and sequence of tenses as students work on the practice activities. Refer back to the boxes on pages 322 and 324 as needed.

## Reteaching (as required)

❑ If students had difficulty with any of the book activities, reteach the section and have students redo the activities.

## Extension and Enrichment (as desired)

❑ Share the NOTES CULTURELLES, TE page 325, about municipal governments in French cities. Students can make comparisons to local governments.

❑ For expansion activities, direct students to www.mcdougallittell.com.

❑ Students can read the short story in *Lecture: Les pêches*, pages 327–332, for enjoyment, or read any of the *Interlude culturel 8* selections, pages 334–343, for information.

❑ Have students do the **Block Schedule Activity** at the top of page 66 of these lesson plans.

## Summary and Closure

❑ Use **Overhead Visuals** Transparency 47. Ask students to talk about what they would like to do or where they would like to go if they were in France. As students share their ideas, guide others in the class to summarize the communicative and linguistic goals demonstrated.

❑ *Lecture (Les pêches):* Read the description of André Theuriet and the historical setting of the story in *Avant de lire*, page 326. Use **Overhead Visuals** Transparency L8 to preview the story as suggested in the TEACHING NOTES on TE page 326. Help students make predictions about the story with *Anticipons un peu!*, page 327. Students can read the story independently or in pairs, stopping after each section to answer the questions in *Avez-vous compris?* and *Anticipons un peu!*. See the TEACHING STRATEGIES and TEACHING NOTES in the TE margins to explain changes in story narration and setting. Use the *Et vous?* and *À votre avis* questions on pages 331–332 to help students suggest what they would have done in the situation and to discuss Vital Herbelot's decision. Use the quiz for *Lecture* in **Reading and Culture Tests and Quizzes**. Choose any or all of the *Après la lecture* oral and written activities on pages 332–333 to conclude the discussion of *Les pêches*.

❏ You may want to use the STUDENT PORTFOLIOS suggestions on TE page 333 to record *Après la lecture* activities for Oral Portfolios.

## Assessment

❏ Use the quiz for *Info Magazine* in **Reading and Culture Tests and Quizzes**. Use the **Unit Quiz** for *Partie 3* as appropriate.

### DAY 4

## Reteaching (as required)

❏ Redo any of the activities in **Practice Activities** that caused students difficulty.

## Assessment

❏ Administer **Unit Test 8** after completing all of the unit's activities. You may also wish to give any or all of the **Proficiency Tests** for the unit: **Listening Comprehension Performance, Speaking Performance**, and **Writing Performance**.

## Notes

# INTERLUDE CULTUREL 8: *Les Antilles francophones*, PAGE 334

## BLOCK SCHEDULE (2 DAYS TO COMPLETE – OPTIONAL)

### Objectives

**Reading Objectives**  To read for content: information about the French-speaking Caribbean islands

To read poetry: *Pour saluer le Tiers-Monde* by Aimé Césaire; *Pour Haïti* by René Depestre

To read a film summary: *Rue Cases-nègres*

**Cultural Objectives**  To learn about important periods and events of the French Antilles

To learn about important people from the Antilles: Joséphine de Beauharnais, Aimé Césaire, Toussaint Louverture

To learn about Haitian art as an expression of life

**Note:** The *Interlude culturel* contains cultural information about the French-speaking Caribbean islands. It can be taught as a lesson or introduced in smaller sections as parts of other lessons. The material can be used to expand cultural awareness, as source material for students' research projects, to develop reading skills, or to build cultural knowledge.

### DAY 1

### Motivation and Focus

❑  Have students preview the pictures on pages 334–343. Encourage them to share what they know about the Caribbean. Use **Overhead Visuals** Transparency 2 to help locate the islands. Read the titles and subtitles on each page. Discuss the people, climate, and geographical region. Who lived on the islands before Europeans arrived? Who are some famous people from the Caribbean islands? How would you describe the art of Haiti? Share the NOTES CULTURELLES, TE page 334.

### Presentation and Explanation

❑  Present an overview of the information on page 334 using **Overhead Visuals** Transparency H5. Have students read page 334. Share the NOTES LINGUISTIQUES in the TE margin. You may want to give students a worksheet such as the one shown on TE page T45 to guide them as they read for information. Discuss the responses. What people came to the islands? Why did they come to the islands? When did some of the islands become independent? Which islands are departments of France?

❑  Have students guess what they will read about on page 335. Explain the NOTE HISTORIQUE and ADDITIONAL INFORMATION in the TE margin. Encourage students to read the selection quickly to find out when the volcano erupted and what the results of the eruption were. Ask students if they believe in curses.

❑  Have students work in small groups to read about the two people on page 336, with half the class reading about Joséphine and the other half reading about Césaire. Ask them to summarize what they learned. You may want to share the NOTE CULTURELLE and ADDITIONAL INFORMATION in the TE margin. Students can look at *Interlude 5*, pages 216–225, for background information on the French Revolution.

❑  Read together about *la négritude*, page 336. Guide students to discover the founders of the movements and their countries of origin. Students can make comparisons between *la négritude* in French-speaking countries and the Black movement in the U.S. Read the poem on page 337 aloud as students follow along in their books. Use the interpretation of the poem in the TEACHING NOTE on TE page 337 to guide student discussion of the feelings and events being described.

❑  Have students read page 338 to find out about Toussaint Louverture. Guide discussion of the events leading up to the revolt, Louverture's role in the revolution, and the outcome. Share the ADDITIONAL INFORMATION and NOTE CULTURELLE on TE page 338. Students may want to compare Toussaint Louverture to a past or contemporary Black American leader.

## Guided Practice and Checking Understanding

❏   You may want to check understanding of these readings by asking students to do a short oral summary of each section. Guide other students to add information as needed.

## Motivation and Focus

❏   Students can begin a project based on *Interlude culturel 8*. Help them begin to research a topic such as a historical event, a famous person, or art from the region.

## Presentation and Explanation

❏   Read and discuss the introduction to the poem on page 339. Encourage students to comment on feelings that exiles might experience. Read the poem aloud as students follow along in their books. Guide students to summarize the content and identify the theme of the poem. You may want to use the TEACHING NOTE suggestion on TE page 339 to compare this poem to *Liberté* on page 257.

❏   Ask students to describe the paintings on pages 340–341; use the TEACHING STRATEGY, TE page 340. As students read the pages, guide discussion of the styles, colors, and content of the pictures. Share information from the NOTES CULTURELLES and NOTE HISTORIQUE on TE pages 340–341.

❏   Use the photos on page 343 to preview the film *Rue Cases-nègres*. See the TEACHING NOTES, TE page 342, and the information on TE page T50 for suggestions and cautions about using the film in class. Read and discuss the film summary on page 342 and the photo captions on page 343. Share the NOTES CULTURELLES, TE pages 342–343.

## Independent Practice

❏   Have students read the selections independently. Students can choose their favorite person, poem, or picture and write a short paragraph explaining why it is their favorite.

## Monitoring and Adjusting

❏   Monitor students' understanding of the readings and cultural content. If students had difficulty in discussions, reread portions aloud and restate the information.

## Reteaching (as required)

❏   Have students review any sections that they found difficult. Provide background knowledge and vocabulary explanations to help them understand the readings.

## Extension and Enrichment (as desired)

❏   Students may wish to research legends of the Caribbean, or other French-speaking islands not presented in the *Interlude*.
❏   For expansion activities, direct students to www.mcdougallittell.com.

## Summary and Closure

❏   Students can present their research and group projects to the class. Help students summarize what they have learned about French-speaking Caribbean islands.
❏   Do the STUDENT PORTFOLIOS suggestion on TE page 339 to have students write and illustrate their own short poems.

## Assessment (optional)

❑　Use **Reading and Culture Tests and Quizzes** for *Interlude culturel 8* to assess students' understanding of the information in this section.

## Notes

# UNITÉ 9: *Les relations personnelles, Partie 1,* PAGE 344

## BLOCK SCHEDULE (3 DAYS TO COMPLETE)

### Objectives

| | |
|---|---|
| **Communication Functions and Contexts** | To talk about friends and acquaintances |
| | To describe friendship |
| | To express feelings toward other people |
| | To congratulate, comfort, and express sympathy for other people |
| **Linguistic Goals** | To use reflexive verbs to describe how people interact with each other |
| | To use relative clauses to describe people and things in complex sentences |
| **Reading and Cultural Objectives** | To learn what friendship and family life mean to the French |
| | To learn what young people in France do to help the disadvantaged |
| | To read for information |

> **Block Schedule**
>
> **Change of Pace** Have students describe a family member's wedding they have attended recently. If they haven't been to one, have them describe a celebrity's wedding or create an imaginary wedding to describe.

**DAY 1**

### Motivation and Focus

❏ *Unit Opener:* Have students look through the photos and pictures on pages 344–357 to preview the unit's content. Read *Thème et Objectifs* and discuss the importance of friends and family. Based on the photos, how are French and American families similar? How are they different?

### Presentation and Explanation

❏ *Le français pratique (Les amis, les copains et les relations personnelles):* Model and have students repeat the expressions in the boxes on pages 348–350. Use **Overhead Visuals** Transparency 50 as a visual aid. Do the TEACHING STRATEGY: WARM-UP on TE page 348 to discuss the meaning of "friend." Use the TEACHING STRATEGY: WARM-UP on TE page 350 to help students talk about relationships between people.

❏ *Langue et communication (Les verbs réfléchis: sens réciproque):* Present the use of reflexive verbs to express reciprocal action, page 352. Use the TEACHING STRATEGY: WARM-UP on TE page 352 to help students use reciprocal verbs. Explain the NOTES LINGUISTIQUES in the TE margin.

### Guided Practice and Checking Understanding

❏ Show **Overhead Visuals** Transparency 50 and have students do the Review and Practice activities on page A109 to practice using reflexive verbs and expressions for talking about friends.

❏ Have students do activities 1–5 (*le français pratique –* pages 159–162 and *Pratique orale 1* (*langue et communication –* page 162) of **Practice Activities** as you play the **Audio**, Cassette 9, Side 1, or read from the **Cassette Script**, pages 52–54.

### Independent Practice

❏ *Pair activities:* Model the activities on pages 348–353. Arrange students in pairs to practice activities 1–3 and 5 (pages 348–351) and 1–2 (pages 352–353). Students can check their answers in the **Answer Key**. You may want to do the EXPANSION, TE page 351.

❏ *Homework:* Assign activities 4 (page 351) and 3 (page 353).

## DAY 2

### Motivation and Focus

❏ *Info Magazine:* Have students scan the article on page 345 to discover what friendship and family mean to the French. Encourage students to look for cognates and guess meanings from context as they read. Use the Teaching Strategy on TE page 344 to compare and contrast French and American family life. Share the information in the Note culturelle, TE page 345. Read *Nous et les autres* on pages 346–347 to find out how the three teenagers help others. Share information in the Realia Note and Note culturelle in the TE margins. Use the Teaching Strategies on TE pages 346 and 347 to help students talk about their friends and write a profile of themselves or a friend. Read about the qualities of a friend on page 346. Have students do the corresponding activity and *Et vous?*.

❏ Help students begin planning the Interdisciplinary/Community Connections pen pal bank project described on TE page 365.

### Presentation and Explanation

❏ *Langue et communication (Révision: Les pronoms relatifs **qui** et **que**):* Review the use of **qui** and **que** in relative clauses, page 354. Model the examples for students to repeat. Use the Teaching Strategy in the side margin of TE page 354 to help students understand the difference between **qui** and **que**.

❏ *Langue et communication (La construction préposition + pronom relatif):* Explain the forms and use of the preposition + relative pronoun construction, page 355. Model the examples for students to repeat. Explain the Notes linguistiques, TE page 355. You may want to introduce contracted forms of **lequel** in *Allons plus loin* on page 356.

❏ *Langue et communication (Le pronom relatif **dont**):* Present the use of **dont** as a relative pronoun, page 357. After modeling the examples, have students repeat. Use the Teaching Strategy: Warm-Up, TE page 357, to help students use **dont** with the expression **avoir besoin.**

### Guided Practice and Checking Understanding

❏ Have students do *Pratique orale 2–3 (langue et communication – page 162)* of **Practice Activities** as you play the **Audio**, Cassette 9, Side 1 or read from the **Cassette Script**, pages 54–55.

❏ Show **Video** Module 10, or read from the **Video Script**, and have students do any or all of the corresponding activities in the **Video Activity Book**.

### Independent Practice

❏ *Pair activities:* Model the activities on pages 354–357. Arrange students in pairs to practice activities 7 and 9–12 (pages 355–357). Students can check their answers in the **Answer Key**. You may want to do the TEACHING STRATEGY, TE page 356, with activity 8, page 356.

❏ *Homework:* Assign activity 6 (page 355).

❏ *Group activities:* Do activities 5 and 8 on pages 354 and 356 in small groups.

### Monitoring and Adjusting

❏ Have students do the writing activities on pages 87–90 of **Practice Activities**.

❏ As students work on the practice activities, monitor use of relative pronouns, reflexive verbs, and expressions for talking about relationships. Refer to pages 348–357. Use the Teaching Strategies on TE pages 349–355 to meet all students' needs.

## DAY 3

### Reteaching (as required)

❑ Use **Video** Module 10 and the suggestions on TE page 356 to review and focus attention on relative pronouns and reciprocal verbs.

### Extension and Enrichment (as desired)

❑ Introduce the SUPPLEMENTARY VOCABULARY on TE pages 348, 349, and 351. Share and discuss the French proverbs about friends and family found on TE pages 348 and 353.

❑ Have students do the **Block Schedule Activity** at the top of page 72 of these lesson plans.

### Summary and Closure

❑ Use **Overhead Visuals** Transparency 50 and the Goal 1 activity on page A109. Guide students to summarize the communicative and linguistic goals demonstrated.

❑ Activity 4 on page 353 may be used for students' Written Portfolios. See the forms and suggestions in **Portfolio Assessment**.

### Assessment

❑ Use the quiz for *Info Magazine* in **Reading and Culture Tests and Quizzes**. Assess understanding by administering the **Unit Quiz** for *Partie 1*.

### Notes

# UNITÉ 9: *Les relations personnelles, Partie 2,* PAGE 358

## BLOCK SCHEDULE (4 DAYS TO COMPLETE, INCLUDING UNIT TEST)

### Objectives

**Communication Functions and Contexts**   To describe the various phases of a person's life

**Linguistic Goals**   To use relative pronouns to describe people and things in complex sentences

**Reading and Cultural Objectives**   To learn what is involved in planning a wedding in France

To read for enjoyment

To read a short story: *Le bracelet* by Michelle Maurois

---

**Block Schedule**

**Personalizing** Have students choose an elder member of their family to interview. The student will then write a short biography of that person using as much of the vocabulary as possible from p. 360, **Les phases de la vie**. Have volunteers read their biographies to the class.

---

### Motivation and Focus

❏   *Info Magazine:* Have students read pages 358–359. Encourage them to look for cognates and guess meanings from context. Use the TEACHING STRATEGY, TE page 358, to guide discussion of the article. Students can compare French and American marriage customs. Share the NOTES CULTURELLES and ADDITIONAL INFORMATION on TE pages 358–359 if appropriate. Do any or all of the *Et vous?* activities on page 359.

### Presentation and Explanation

❏   *Le français pratique (Les phases de la vie):* Model and have students repeat the expressions on page 360. Use **Overhead Visuals** Transparency 51 as a visual aid. Remind students of the past tense of the verbs **naître** and **mourir**, *Rappel!* box, page 360. Guide students to talk about phases in their own lives.

### Guided Practice and Checking Understanding

❏   Use **Overhead Visuals** Transparency 51 with the Review and Practice activities on page A111 to have students practice using relative pronouns to describe the various stages of life.

❏   Have students do Activities 1–4 (*le français pratique* – pages 163–164) of **Practice Activities** as you play the **Audio**, Cassette 9, Side 2, or read from the **Cassette Script**, pages 55–57.

### Independent Practice

❏   *Pair activities:* Model the activities on pages 361. In pairs, have students practice activities 1–2 (page 361). Students can check their work in the **Answer Key**.

❏   *Homework:* Assign activities 3 and 4 on page 361.

### Presentation and Explanation

❏   *Langue et communication (Résumé: les pronoms relatifs):* Present the chart on relative pronouns, page 362. Guide students to create sentences based on the chart to review the uses of the various relative pronouns. Explain the NOTE LINGUISTIQUE, TE page 362.

❑ *Langue et communication* (**Ce qui, ce que** and **ce dont**): Explain the uses of **ce qui, ce que**, and **ce dont** on page 364. Model the examples for students to repeat and guide them to discuss the forms in the examples. Share the information in NOTES LINGUISTIQUES, TE page 364.

## Guided Practice and Checking Understanding

❑ Have students do *Pratique orale* 1–2 (*langue et communication* – page 164) of **Practice Activities** as you play the **Audio**, Cassette 9, Side 2, or read from the **Cassette Script**, page 57.

❑ Show **Video** Module 11, or read from the **Video Script**, and have students do any or all of the corresponding activities in the **Video Activity Book**.

## Independent Practice

❑ *Pair activities:* Model the activities on pages 362–365. In pairs, have students practice activities 1–2 and 5–6 (pages 362 and 365). Students can check their work in the **Answer Key**.

❑ *Homework:* Assign activity 3 on page 363. As you go over the homework, explain the legend of *Tristan et Yseult* in the NOTES CULTURELLES on TE page 363.

❑ *Group activities:* Students can practice in small groups with activity 4 (page 363).

❑ Do any of the additional activities in **Teacher to Teacher**, pages 105–115.

## Monitoring and Adjusting

❑ Have students do the writing activities on pages 91–94 of **Practice Activities**.

❑ As students work on the practice activities, monitor use of relative pronouns **ce qui, ce que**, and **ce dont**. Check use of vocabulary for stages of life. Refer students to pages 360–364, as needed. Do the TEACHING STRATEGIES on TE pages 360, 361, and 362 to meet all students' needs.

DAY 3

## Reteaching (as required)

❑ If students had difficulty with vocabulary or structures, reteach the section and have students redo the corresponding practice activities in the book.

❑ Use **Video** Module 11 and the suggestions on TE page 356 to review and focus attention on relative pronouns.

## Extension and Enrichment (as desired)

❑ You may want to assign as supplementary reading the short story in *Lecture: Le bracelet*, pages 367–370, or any of the *Interlude* selections on pages 372–381.

❑ Introduce the SUPPLEMENTARY VOCABULARY on TE page 360. Share and discuss the NOTE LINGUISTIQUE and the French proverb about life on TE page 361.

❑ For expansion activities, direct students to www.mcdougallittell.com.

❑ Have students do the **Block Schedule Activity** at the top of page 75 of these lesson plans.

## Summary and Closure

❑ Use the Goal 1 activity on page A111 of **Overhead Visuals** along with Transparency 51. Ask pairs of students to prepare conversations between people on the transparency. Guide other students to summarize the communicative and linguistic goals demonstrated.

❏ *Lecture (Le bracelet):* Use the TEACHING STRATEGY, TE page 366, and *Avant de lire* activities, page 366, along with **Overhead Visuals** Transparency L9 to help students make predictions about the story. Have students read the story on pages 367–370. Students can answer the questions in *Avez-vous compris?* and *Anticipons un peu!* after reading each section of the story. Share the information on TE pages 367–368 as needed: NOTE CULTURELLE, NOTE LINGUISTIQUE, and SUPPLEMENTARY VOCABULARY. Use the TEACHING STRATEGY suggestions on TE pages 368 and 370 to discuss opinions and describe elements of the story. Use the quiz for *Lecture* in **Reading and Culture Tests and Quizzes**. Use any of the oral or written activities in *Après la lecture*, page 371, to conclude discussion of the story.

❏ Do any of the STUDENT PORTFOLIOS suggestions on TE page 371 for preparing a letter and role play for inclusion in Oral and Written Portfolios.

## Assessment

❏ Use the quiz for *Info Magazine* in **Reading and Culture Tests and Quizzes**. Assess understanding by administering the **Unit Quiz** for *Partie 2.*

### DAY 4

## Reteaching

❏ Redo any of the activities in **Practice Activities** that caused students difficulty.

## Assessment

❏ Administer **Unit Test 9** after completing all of the unit's activities. You may also wish to give any or all of the **Proficiency Tests** for the unit: **Listening Comprehension Performance**, **Speaking Performance**, and **Writing Performance**.

## Notes

# INTERLUDE CULTUREL 9: *L'Afrique dans la communauté francophone,* PAGE 372

## BLOCK SCHEDULE (2 DAYS TO COMPLETE – OPTIONAL)

### Objectives

**Reading Objectives**　To read for content: information about the place of Western and Central Africa in the Francophone world

To read an African fable: *La gélinotte et la tortue*

To read a poem: *Afrique* by David Diop

To read an African legend: *La légende baoulé* by Bernard Dadié

**Cultural Objectives**　To learn about important periods and events of African history: prehistory, the African empires, colonization and independence

To learn basic facts about Western Africa: the people, their language and culture, their religions and traditions

To learn about African art and its influence on European art

**Note:** The *Interlude culturel* contains cultural information about Africa. It can be taught as a lesson or introduced in smaller sections as parts of other lessons. The material in this section can be used to expand cultural awareness, as source material for students' research projects, to develop reading skills, or to build cultural knowledge.

### DAY 1

### Motivation and Focus

❑　Have students look through the pictures on pages 372–381 for names of African countries in the captions, titles, and subtitles of the *Interlude*. Show **Overhead Visuals** Transparency 4 and have students find countries. Encourage them to comment on the people, art, and architecture shown in the pictures and share information they may know about African history and culture.

### Presentation and Explanation

❑　Use **Overhead Visuals** Transparency H6 as you give an oral preview of pages 372–373. Present the different time periods and empires on the time line. What do the pictures show about these time periods? What does the art tell you about the culture of the people? Have students read pages 372–373 to find out more information about the time periods and empire. Guide discussion of the reading. Share the NOTES HISTORIQUES, NOTES CULTURELLES, and ADDITIONAL INFORMATION in the TE margins. Help students summarize the major events of each of the periods.

❑　Introduce the selections on Francophone Africa and its culture on pages 374–377. Together, read the first question and paragraph on page 374. Help students locate the countries mentioned on a map (**Overhead Visuals** Transparency 4 or textbook *Appendix D* page R37). Encourage students to suggest why these countries continue to use French as their administrative and commercial language.

❑　Have students read pages 374–377 as a cooperative group activity. Divide the class into six "expert" groups and have each group read and discuss one aspect of culture. Then regroup so that each new group contains one member of each "expert" group, who teaches that group's information to the others. Summarize as a whole class, sharing the information from the NOTES CULTURELLES, NOTE HISTORIQUE, NOTES LINGUISTIQUES, ANECDOTE, ADDITIONAL INFORMATION, and PHOTO NOTE on TE pages 374–377.

### Guided Practice and Checking Understanding

❑　You may check understanding of the readings by asking students to do a short oral summary of each selection. Help other students add information to the summaries.

## DAY 2

### Motivation and Focus

❏ Students can begin a project based on the *Interlude culturel*. Projects can focus on different disciplines such as art, history, sociology, or anthropology. Students may prefer to research one of the empires or aspects of culture presented in the *Interlude*.

### Presentation and Explanation

❏ Students can read the African fable on page 377. Help them identify and describe the **gélinotte** and the **tortue**. Why did the grouse think he was better? What happened on the plains? Who survived? What is the moral of the story? Students can compare the African fable to other fables they know or have read.

❏ Present the information about David Diop on page 378. Read the poem *Afrique* as students follow along in their books. Use the TEACHING STRATEGY, TE page 378, to help students analyze the poem. Share the information about the baobab tree in the NOTE CULTURELLE, TE page 378.

❏ Ask students to describe the masks and pictures on page 379. What similarities do they notice between the African masks and the statue and painting by European artists? Have students read page 379. Guide discussion of the role of sculpture in African culture and how African art influenced 20th century European artists and the cubist art movement. Discuss the information in the NOTE CULTURELLE and ADDITIONAL INFORMATION on TE page 379.

❏ Together, read the information about Bernard Dadié on page 380. Have students read the legend independently or in pairs to find out how the Baoulé tribe got its name. Guide students to retell the legend. Explain the NOTE CULTURELLE, TE page 380.

### Independent Practice

❏ Have students reread the selections independently. Ask them to choose an aspect of African culture from those presented in the readings and write a short paragraph explaining what they learned about African culture and why it is interesting to them.

❏ Use the TEACHING STRATEGY at the bottom of TE page 381 to have students write and illustrate a legend.

### Monitoring and Adjusting

❏ Use the TEACHING STRATEGY in the side margin of TE page 381 to monitor students' understanding of the Baoulé legend. Help students analyze the legend. Guide students to go back through the reading to find specific details to support their answers.

### Reteaching (as required)

❏ Have students review any sections that they found difficult. Provide background knowledge and vocabulary explanations to help them understand the readings.

### Extension and Enrichment (as desired)

❏ Students may wish to research specific countries in Francophone Africa or one of the African empires mentioned in the *Interlude*.
❏ For expansion activities, direct students to www.mcdougallittell.com.

### Summary and Closure

❏ Have students share with the class the results of their projects or research about Francophone Africa. As students make their presentations, help them summarize what they have learned about African culture.

### Assessment (optional)

❏ Use **Reading and Culture Tests and Quizzes** for *Interlude culturel 9* to assess students' understanding of the information in this section.

# UNITÉ 10: *Vers la vie active, Partie 1,* PAGE 382

## BLOCK SCHEDULE (3 DAYS TO COMPLETE)

### Objectives

| | |
|---|---|
| **Communication Functions and Contexts** | To talk about what you plan to study in the future |
| | To discuss jobs and professions and plan for a career |
| **Linguistic Goals** | To use the preposition + infinitive construction with *pour*, *sans*, and *avant de* |
| | To use the past infinitive after *après* to describe an action that occurs before another action |
| | To use the present participle to describe simultaneous actions |
| | To use the present participle to indicate why you do certain things |
| **Reading and Cultural Objectives** | To learn how important academic success is to French young people |
| | To learn which are the most popular professions in France |
| | To read for information |

> **Block Schedule**
>
> **Peer Review** Have students work in pairs to begin making flashcards with the name of a profession on one side and the principle activity on the other; for example: **vétérinaire/soigner les animaux, professeur/ enseigner.** Students should cover the professions they know so far and add to the flashcards as they move through the Unit.

### DAY 1

### Motivation and Focus

❑ *Unit Opener:* Have students look through the photos and realia on pages 382–385. Read the *Thème et Objectifs* and ask students to predict the content of the unit. Guide discussion of how young people prepare for life after graduation. What options are available for French and American young people?

### Presentation and Explanation

❑ *Le français pratique (Études ou travail?):* Use **Overhead Visuals** Transparencies 9 and 52 to introduce the names of studies and professions shown in the boxes on pages 386–387. Model the vocabulary and expressions for students to repeat. Do the TEACHING STRATEGY: WARM-UP, TE page 387, to help students identify names of professions with work places.

❑ *Langue et communication (La construction préposition + infinitif):* Present the use of the infinitive forms after the prepositions **pour**, **sans**, and **avant de**, page 388. Model the examples for students to repeat. Use the TEACHING STRATEGY at the bottom of TE page 388 to help students use the construction to talk about themselves, friends, or family.

### Guided Practice and Checking Understanding

❑ Use **Overhead Visuals** Transparency 9 to help students practice talking about different jobs. Practice talking about future studies and careers with Transparency 52 and the activities on page A114.

❑ Have students do activities 1–4 (*le français pratique* – pages 165–166) and *Pratique orale* 1 (*langue et communication* – page 167) of **Practice Activities** as you play the **Audio**, Cassette 10, Side 1, or read from the **Cassette Script**, pages 58–60.

### Independent Practice

❑ *Pair activities:* Model the activities on pages 386–388. Students can work in pairs on activities 2–3 (page 387) and 1–3 (page 388). Have students check their work using the **Answer Key**. You may want to do the EXPANSION suggestions on TE pages 387 and 388.

❑ *Group activities:* Students can practice in small groups with activity 1 on page 386.

## DAY 2

### Motivation and Focus

❏ *Info Magazine:* Students can read pages 383–384. Encourage them to read for general understanding of what the *bac* is and what it means to French young people. Share information in the NOTES CULTURELLES and NOTES LINGUISTIQUES on TE pages 382–385. Read page 385, sharing the ADDITIONAL INFORMATION about the military service in the TE margin. Do *Et vous?*, pages 384 and 385.

❏ Students may want to begin planning a career day, as described on TE page 401 in INTERDISCIPLINARY/COMMUNITY CONNECTIONS. Students can work in small groups researching professions in different fields that involve foreign languages.

### Presentation and Explanation

❏ *Langue et communication (L'infinitif passé):* Introduce the forms and uses of the past infinitive, page 389. Explain the information in NOTES LINGUISTIQUES, TE page 389.

❏ *Langue et communication (Le participe présent):* Present the forms and uses of the present participle on page 390. Model the examples for students to repeat. Introduce the three irregular verb forms for the present participle. Use the TEACHING STRATEGY: MULTIPLE INTELLIGENCES, TE page 390, to help students transform sentences and use the present participle.

### Guided Practice and Checking Understanding

❏ Have students do *Pratique orale 3 (langue et communication* – page 167) of **Practice Activities** as you play the **Audio**, Cassette 10, Side 1, or read from the **Cassette Script**, page 60.

❏ Show the Mise en scène and Problème! sections of **Video** Module 12, or read from the **Video Script**, and have students do the corresponding activities in the **Video Activity Book**.

### Independent Practice

❏ *Pair activities:* Model the activities on pages 389–391. Students can work in pairs on activities 5 and 7–10. Have students check their work using the **Answer Key**. You may want to do the VARIATION suggestion on TE page 391.

❏ *Homework:* Assign activities 4 (page 389) and 6 (page 390).

❏ Do any of the additional activities in **Teacher to Teacher**, pages 116–118.

### Monitoring and Adjusting

❏ Have students do the writing activities on pages 95–100 of **Practice Activities**.

❏ As students work on the practice activities, monitor use of past infinitives, present participles, preposition and infinitive constructions, and names of professions and studies. Refer to pages 386–390 as needed. Do the TEACHING STRATEGY and NOTES LINGUISTIQUES on TE page 386.

## DAY 3

### Reteaching (as required)

❏ Reteach portions of the lesson as needed. Explain the NOTES LINGUISTIQUES, TE page 386, to help students talk about professions. Use the TEACHING STRATEGY: ADDITIONAL PRACTICE, TE page 390, for practicing present participles.

### Extension and Enrichment (as desired)

❏ You may want to introduce the SUPPLEMENTARY VOCABULARY on TE page 387 to help students talk about other professions. Present and guide discussion of the PROVERBE, TE page 387, and the saying in the NOTE CULTURELLE, TE page 388.

❏   For expansion activities, direct students to www.mcdougallittell.com.
❏   Have students do the **Block Schedule Activity** at the top of page 80 of these lesson plans.

## Summary and Closure

❏   Show **Overhead Visuals** Transparency 52. Ask students to choose one of the ads and give reasons why they would or would not like to attend the school. Have other students summarize the communicative and linguistic goals demonstrated.

## Assessment

❏   Use the quiz for *Info Magazine* in **Reading and Culture Tests and Quizzes**. Assess understanding of each part of the lesson by administering the **Unit Quiz** for *Partie 1*.

## Notes

# UNITÉ 10: *Vers la vie active, Partie 2,* PAGE 392

## BLOCK SCHEDULE (4 DAYS TO COMPLETE, INCLUDING UNIT TEST)

### Objectives

**Communication Functions and Contexts**
To indicate what type of job or profession you would like to have

To be able to look for a job

To describe your personal qualifications

To prepare a résumé in French

**Linguistic Goals**
To use conjunction + subjunctive to explain the purpose, conditions or restrictions, or time limitations of an action

**Reading and Cultural Objectives**
To learn how to prepare for an interview with a French company

To read for information and enjoyment

To read a short story: *Le portrait* by Yves Thériault

> ### Block Schedule
> **Change of Pace** Have students work in small groups and create a Help Wanted page. Students should write and design a minimum of 8 job ads and lay them out on a piece of paper. Display the "newspapers" on the bulletin board.

### DAY 1

### Motivation and Focus

❑ *Info Magazine:* Ask students to describe the illustrations and photos on pages 392–393 and share experiences they have had with job interviews. Have students read pages 392–393, using the TEACHING STRATEGY at the bottom of TE page 393. Explain the NOTES CULTURELLES. Do the TEACHING STRATEGY, TE page 392, to role play interview situations. Students can do the *Et vous?* activities on page 393.

### Presentation and Explanation

❑ *Le français pratique (La vie professionnelle):* Model the expressions for describing professional life, page 394, for students to repeat. Talk about their future professional plans. Begin the TEACHING STRATEGY, TE page 394, to prepare a curriculum vitae.

❑ *Le français pratique (À la recherche d'un emploi):* Present the interview questions and answers on pages 396–397. Have students repeat. Guide them to talk about their own job interests and skills. Share the information in the NOTES CULTURELLES and NOTE LINGUISTIQUE, TE pages 396–397.

### Guided Practice and Checking Understanding

❑ Show **Overhead Visuals** Transparency 53 and have students practice asking and answering questions about the ads as described on page A117.

❑ Have students do Activities 1–5 (*le français pratique* – pages 168–171) of **Practice Activities** as you play the **Audio**, Cassette 10, Side 2, or read from the **Cassette Script**, pages 60–63.

### Independent Practice

❑ *Pair activities:* Model the activities on pages 395–397. Students can practice activities 2–3 (page 395) and *Conversations libres* (page 397) in pairs. Have students check their work in the **Answer Key**. You may want to do the TEACHING STRATEGY and EXPANSION suggestions, TE page 395.

❑ *Homework:* Assign activity 1 (page 395).

❑ Do any or all of the activities in **Teacher to Teacher**, pages 119–129.

## DAY 2

### Presentation and Explanation

❏ *Langue et communication (La construction conjonction + subjonctif):* Introduce the use of the subjunctive after certain conjunctions, page 398. Model the examples for students to repeat. Use the TEACHING STRATEGY, TE page 398, to help students create sentences using the conjunctions and the subjunctive.

### Guided Practice and Checking Understanding

❏ Have students do *Pratique orale* 1-2 (*langue et communication* – page 172) of **Practice Activities** as you play the **Audio**, Cassette 10, Side 2, or read from the **Cassette Script**, pages 63–64.
❏ Review **Video** Module 12. Show the Problème! section, or read the **Video Script**, and have students do the Problème! and Supplément activities in the **Video Activity Book**.

### Independent Practice

❏ *Pair activities:* Model the activities on pages 399–401. Students can practice activities 3–7 in pairs. Have students check their work in the **Answer Key**.
❏ *Homework:* Assign activities 1–2 (page 399).
❏ *Group activities:* Students can practice activity 8 (page 401) in small groups.

### Monitoring and Adjusting

❏ Have students do the writing activities on pages 101–104 of **Practice Activities**.
❏ Monitor use of the subjunctive and interview expressions as students work on the practice activities. Refer back to the boxes on pages 394–398 as needed. Use the NOTES LINGUISTIQUES on TE pages 394–398.

## DAY 3

### Reteaching (as required)

❏ Reteach any of the structures or expressions that students found difficult and redo the corresponding book activities.

### Extension and Enrichment (as desired)

❏ You may want to introduce the SUPPLEMENTARY VOCABULARY on TE pages 395–397. Help students use the vocabulary to talk about job interests and experience. Share the information in the NOTE CULTURELLE, TE page 394, and EXPANSION LINGUISTIQUE, TE page 401. Encourage students to compare French and American business and job information.
❏ Students may read the *Lecture: Le portrait*, pages 403–408, or any of the selections from *Interlude culturel 10*, pages 410–420, for enrichment.

### Summary and Closure

❏ Show **Overhead Visuals** Transparency 53. Do the Goal 1 activities on page A118 to have students practice job interviews and talking about job preferences. Guide others to summarize the communicative and linguistic goals demonstrated.
❏ *Lecture (Le portrait):* Use the TEACHING STRATEGY, TE page 402, and *Avant de lire* activities, page 402, with **Overhead Visuals** Transparency L10 to help students make predictions about the story. Optionally, do the TEACHING STRATEGY, TE page 403, to have students prepare captions for the story before reading. Have students read the story on pages 403–408. Students can answer the questions in *Avez-vous compris?* and *Anticipons un peu!* after reading each section of the story. Share the information on TE

pages 402–408 as needed: NOTE CULTURELLE, NOTES LINGUISTIQUES, and ADDITIONAL INFORMATION. Use the TEACHING STRATEGY suggestions on TE pages 405, 407, and 408 to describe the portrait and to summarize the outcome of the story. Give the quiz for *Lecture* in **Reading and Culture Tests and Quizzes**. Use any of the activities in *Après la lecture*, page 409, to conclude discussion of the story.

❏ You may want to use any of the suggestions in STUDENT PORTFOLIOS, TE page 409, recording the *Situations*, page 409, or *Conversations libres*, page 397, for students' Oral Portfolios; use *Expression écrite*, page 409, for Written Portfolios.

## Assessment

❏ Use the quiz for *Info Magazine* in **Reading and Culture Tests and Quizzes**. Assess understanding by administering the **Unit Quiz** for *Partie 2*.

## Reteaching (as required)

❏ Redo any of the activities in **Practice Activities** that caused students difficulty.

## Assessment

❏ Administer **Unit Test 10** after completing the unit. Give any or all of the **Proficiency Tests**: **Listening Comprehension Performance**, **Speaking Performance**, and **Writing Performance**.

# INTERLUDE CULTUREL 10: *La France et le Nouveau Monde,* PAGE 410

## BLOCK SCHEDULE (2 DAYS TO COMPLETE – OPTIONAL)

### Objectives

**Reading Objectives**    To read for content: information about the French presence in North America

To read a song: *Réveille* by Zachary Richard

To read a letter: *Lettre à sa femme* by La Fayette

**Cultural Objectives**    To learn about the important events in the history of the French in Canada and Louisiana

To learn about important people: Jacques Cartier, Jeanne Mance, Cavelier de La Salle

To learn about important groups of people: Huguenots, Escadrille Lafayette, Acadiens (Cajuns), Creoles

To learn why certain American cities have French names

**Note:** The *Interlude culturel* contains cultural information about France and the New World. It can be taught as a lesson or introduced in smaller sections as parts of other lessons. The material in this section can be used to expand cultural awareness, as source material for students' research projects, to develop reading skills, or to build cultural knowledge.

### DAY 1

## Motivation and Focus

❏   Have students preview the pictures on pages 410–420. Ask them if they are familiar with any of the people or events represented in the pictures. Read the titles and subtitles on each page. Use **Overhead Visuals** Transparency H5 to give an overview of the role of France in North America. What explorers do students know from history? What cities did the French found? What leaders were important? What areas of North America retain aspects of French culture?

## Presentation and Explanation

❏   Preview the selections on French exploration in the New World on pages 410–411. Use **Overhead Visuals** Transparencies H5 and 3 to point out places and events. Ask students to read the pages to find the answers to the three questions in the subtitles. Guide discussion of the answers. Share the information in the NOTES CULTURELLES, PHOTO NOTES, and NOTE LINGUISTIQUE, TE pages 410–411. Encourage students to describe characteristics, qualities, or skills needed to be an explorer or settler.

❏   Point out important events on Transparency H5 during the time periods of *la Nouvelle France* and *la guerre d'Indépendance*. Have students read pages 412–413 to find out the extent of French territory in the New World, the role of France in the two wars, and who the Huguenots were. Share the information in the TE margin notes. Help students summarize the information that they found.

❏   Have students read about La Fayette on page 414 and the letter to his wife on page 415. Guide discussion of La Fayette's role in the American Revolutionary War and in the French Revolution. Share the NOTES HISTORIQUES in the TE margin. What was La Fayette's impression of the American people? How did he describe American life? Would people visiting America today get the same impression? Why or why not?

## Guided Practice and Checking Understanding

❏   You may check understanding of these readings by asking students to do a short summary of each section. Help other students add information to the summaries.

## Motivation and Focus

❑ Students may want to begin a project based on the *Interlude culturel*. Students may do the INTERDISCIPLINARY/COMMUNITY CONNECTIONS project, TE page 417, to create a time line charting France's role in American history, or research a person or group of people presented in the *Interlude*.

## Presentation and Explanation

❑ Use the pictures and captions on page 416 to preview the French–American connection during World Wars I and II. You may want to use the TEACHING STRATEGY suggestion on TE page 416 to guide reading of the selections. Share the information in the NOTES CULTURELLES in the TE margin.

❑ Have students read about the origin of French names of American cities and French heritage in Louisiana on pages 417–418. Ask students to explain the stories behind the city names. Discuss the NOTES HISTORIQUES on TE page 417. Students can refer to the map of **la Nouvelle France** on page 412 and discuss why most of the French names are near the Mississippi River. Help students summarize the story of the Acadians and the origin of **créole** on page 418. Share the NOTES CULTURELLES and POUR EN SAVOIR PLUS information on TE pages 418–419.

❑ Read aloud *Réveille*, page 419, as students follow along in their books. If possible, play a recording of the song, as suggested in TEACHING STRATEGY, TE page 419. Help students describe the poem's tone and mood. What historical events are mentioned in the poem?

❑ Have students read about the Acadian flag on page 420. Help students explain the symbols and colors of the flag. What historical events are related on the flag? Share the NOTES CULTURELLES and ADDITIONAL INFORMATION in the TE margin.

## Independent Practice

❑ Have students reread the selections independently. Ask them to choose a favorite event, person, or group presented in the readings and write a paragraph explaining the significance of the person or event in the history of North America.

## Monitoring and Adjusting

❑ As students participate in discussions about the reading selections, monitor their understanding of the events. If students are having difficulty, help them look back through the readings for information.

## Reteaching (as required)

❑ Have students review any sections that they found difficult. Provide background knowledge and vocabulary explanations to help them understand the readings.

## Extension and Enrichment (as desired)

❑ Students may wish to research other topics related to *Interlude culturel 10*: other American cities/states with French names, Cajun and Creole culture, famous people of Creole descent, or other French explorers.

❑ For expansion activities, direct students to www.mcdougallittell.com.

## Summary and Closure

❑ Students can share with the class the results of their interdisciplinary projects or their research about one of the people or groups mentioned in the *Interlude*. As students make their presentations, help them summarize what they have learned about the role and influence of France in North American history.

## Assessment (optional)

❑ Use **Reading and Culture Tests and Quizzes** for *Interlude culturel 10* to assess students' understanding of the information in this section.

## Notes